Nostalgic Memories of HUDDERSFIELD

The publishers would like to thank the following companies for their support in the production of this book

Main sponsor

Syngenta

Armitage Sykes LLP
Bower Roebuck Ltd
Crowther & Shaw
Cummins Turbo Technologies
J & E Dickinson - Longley Farm
H Downs & Son
Dugdale Bros. Ltd
Garrards
Holmfirth Dyers Ltd
W T Johnson & Sons
Kirklees College
Longley Park Motors Ltd
Myers Group
Nelson Roller & Rubber Company
Pearson Funeral Service
Phoenox Textiles Ltd
Richard Carter Ltd
J B Schofield & Sons
Taylor & Lodge
Wood Auto Supplies Ltd

First published in Great Britain by True North Books Limited
England HX3 6SN
01422 244555

www.truenorthbooks.com

ISBN 978 - 1906649692

Text, design and origination by True North Books
Printed and bound by Charlesworth Press

Nostalgic Memories of HUDDERSFIELD

CONTENTS

INTRODUCTION

Such has been the popularity of our previous books on the Huddersfield area, that we have been encouraged to produce a new publication. Our books allow readers to walk on cobbled streets, browse in well known local shops of the period and revisit special events and occasions, without leaving the comfort of their favourite armchair.

'Change' is relentless and in some parts of the area the transformation will be more obvious than others. Huddersfield town centre and the roads around it have changed significantly from times gone by. Some of the older and architecturally impressive buildings have retained their originality on the outside, although their uses have changed.

The title of this new book, 'Nostalgic Memories of Huddersfield', tells you all you need to know about what is captured within its pages. Turning over leaf after leaf will bring you to a treasure trove from the last century. Through the images and thoughtful text, the reader is taken on a steam train ride back through the mists of time to an age when dad could buy a suit at the Fifty Shilling Tailor and when variety theatre and ballroom dancing was all the rage. Perhaps you visited the Palace Theatre music hall which later became the The Palace Continental, or remember the frenzied excitement of The Beatles concert at the ABC Cinema in 1963.

We make no apologies for the fact that some of the photographs will be outside living memory because they will still be familiar to us. They may feature an event described to us by a close relative or they could feature historical landmarks such as bridges and buildings.

Whatever the view taken on the boundaries that separate 'history', 'nostalgia' or 'the present', we should all invest a little time occasionally to reflect on the past and the people and events which helped to shape life as we know it today.

TEXT — ANDREW MITCHELL, STEVE AINSWORTH, BRENDAN O' NEILL
PHOTOGRAPH RESEARCH — BRENDAN O' NEILL
DESIGNER — SEAMUS MOLLOY
BUSINESS DEVELOPMENT MANAGER — ANDREW HALES

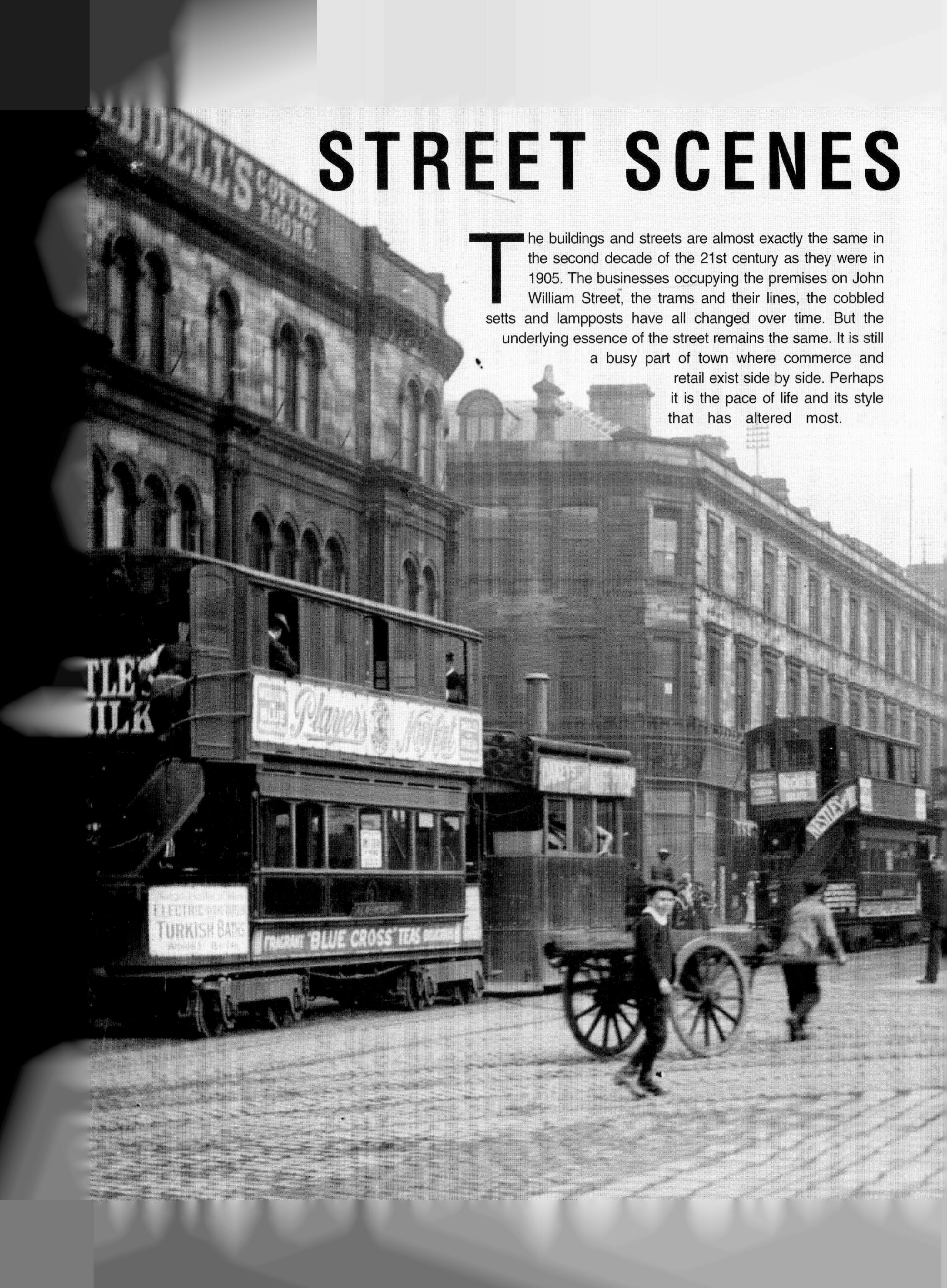

STREET SCENES

The buildings and streets are almost exactly the same in the second decade of the 21st century as they were in 1905. The businesses occupying the premises on John William Street, the trams and their lines, the cobbled setts and lampposts have all changed over time. But the underlying essence of the street remains the same. It is still a busy part of town where commerce and retail exist side by side. Perhaps it is the pace of life and its style that has altered most.

Despite the coming of the tram service, the roads were still basically places where people walked, cycled or used horses and carts. Ladies' fashions, in particular, hinted at this more sedate manner. They wore dresses and skirts that touched the pavements beneath their feet. Above the waistline, they favoured high necks to their blouses and would seldom be seen in public without a fine hat or bonnet. This was often set on top of a 'Gibson girl' hairstyle. Although women's clothing was still similar to that favoured in late Victorian times, by the end of the Edwardian decade a straighter, columnal style was evolving. Before long, fashionable ladies would abandon the corset as an indispensable garment. Men were slow to change. Nothing new there, you might say. Even so, there was a move towards more practical wear as the lounge coat replaced the frock coat and three piece suits became more popular. Of course, such items were the province of the middle classes as the lower ranks wore what they could afford.

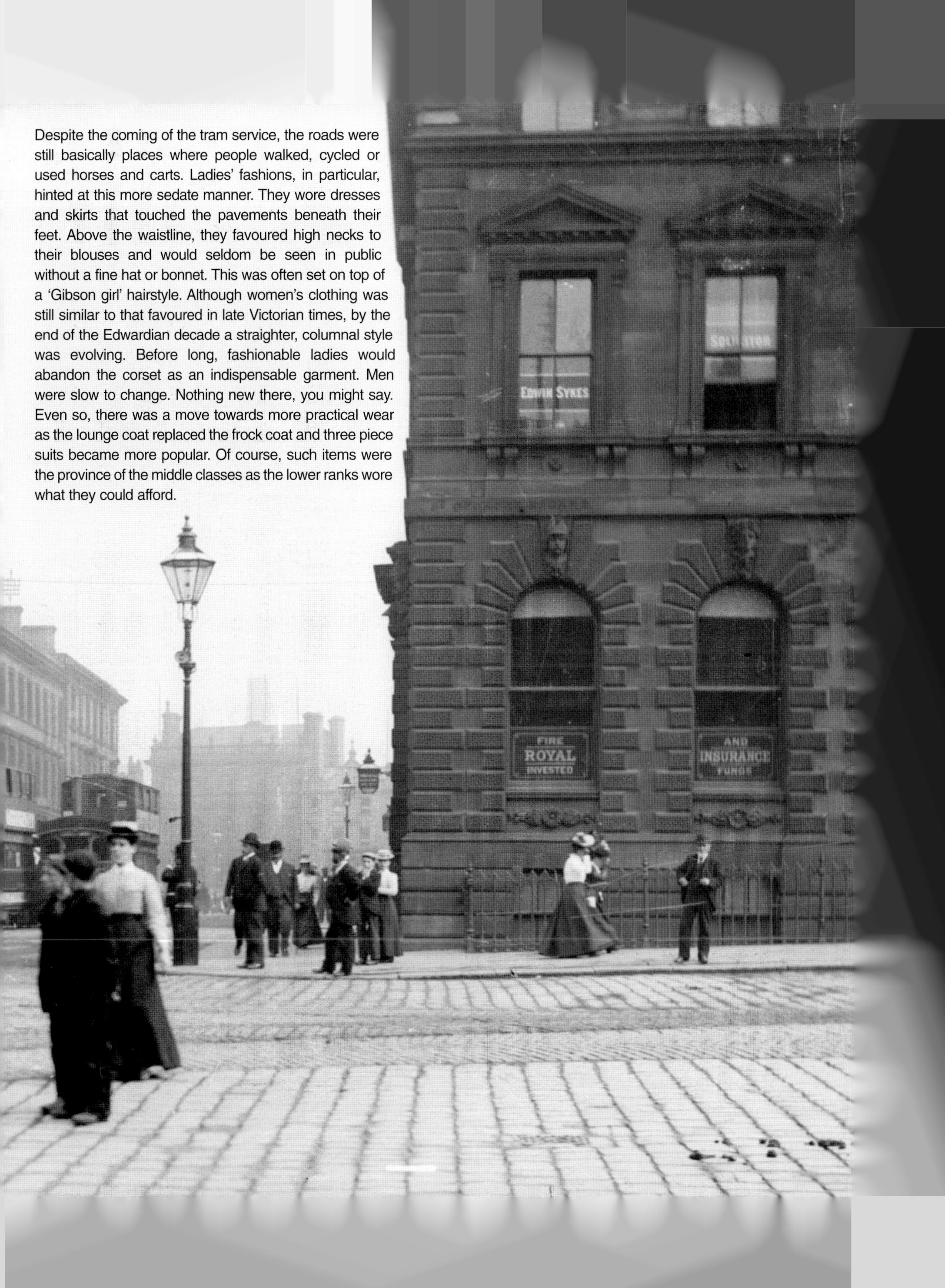

Above: This is an older photo of Cross Church Street in 1885 and we can still make out the overall layout of the street including the White Lion Hotel and the Sun Inn next to each other on the right. A man can be seen to the left of the horse and cart, carrying a double billboard possibly advertising the products of a local shop.

Bottom left: The horse drawn taxicabs hovered near the railway station on St George's Square. This was the very last year of the 19th century and, as the drivers waited patiently for a fare, most thoughts turned to what the new century would bring. The current one had been dominated by the industrial revolution and the development of great trade markets overseas. Travel had been revolutionised by the railways and the age of steam had helped move workers from the land and into towns. Often, families uprooted from places where they had lived for generations before and decamped on the other side of the country. Others had wider horizons and emigrated to America, Canada and Australia. The cabbies looked out across the liberal amount of horse droppings on the square to the Lion Arcade buildings. With the eponymous creature standing on top of the collection of shops, offices and storage facilities, these were the visible testament of the prosperity achieved by the wool manufacturers and merchants. Designed by the York based James Pigott Pritchett, the Lion Arcade was constructed by Samuel Oldfield. St George's Square and its perimeter buildings date from the period 1846-59. This was part of the Ramsden family's hopes of creating a 'new town' with the advent of the railway here. The Ramsdens wanted to ensure that visitors would be impressed with Huddersfield as they left the station, so they took great pains to have top class buildings put up on the fringes of the square.

Above: Sergeantson Street meets Half Moon Street at a spot where there now are several restaurants serving tasty Asian foods. Such establishments were unknown to diners in 1930. How things change. That phrase could almost be the title for this photograph. The horse and carriage was the way for a man to get about town in his dad's era. In what was then the modernity of the interwar era, the shiny motorcar was the thing to own. It could whiz along the open road at high speed as well as negotiating the high streets of our towns and cities with reasonable ease. Britain had a flourishing automobile industry. Austin, Morris and Rolls Royce were names which immediately spring to mind, but there were many others that enjoyed spells of popularity and prosperity. Crossley's was one such company. Established by brothers Francis and William in 1867 in Manchester, it manufactured pumps, presses and small steam engines. The Crossley brothers experimented with building four stroke oil fired engines and the company then moved on to the petrol driven ones. The first Crossley car was manufactured in 1904. A large factory site was purchased in the Stockport area and the years after the First World War saw production of upmarket vehicles rapidly expand. Although its car production continued until the start of the next war, Crossley's began to concentrate on developing its manufacture of buses. The company was taken over by AEC in 1948, though the Crossley name continued in use into the 1950s.

Did you know?

Huddersfield probably means "The Field of an Englishman called Huthhere, or of a Scandinavian called Hather".

Above: An image of the Huddersfield Railway Station at the turn of the century, showing the coal carts to the right being pulled by shire horses and the more sedate carriages to the left dropping their passengers off for the next leg of their journey. We have been unable to ascertain the role of the 'kiosk' in the centre of the photo but it may well have been an early information booth for travellers.

Bottom left: The Commercial Hotel in Buxton Road is situated on a busy corner just off New Street. The Policeman in the white coat directs an assortment of vehicles including cars, wagons, trams and horses and carts, it does seem a difficult job, particularly at a busy time.

Below: The Ramsden Estate Buildings still cuts an imposing sight on the corner of Westgate, just as they did back in 1910. Then, it was a mixture of horse drawn vehicles and trams that passed by its doors, with only a handful of cars or small trucks chugging by. The centre of the town was developed as an area of handsome commercial buildings. The grandeur of the structures and ornate nature of the decoration and design reflected the wealth and importance of those for whom they were built. The economic stability and growth during the mid to late 19th century yielded us some of the most handsome edifices we could ever wish to have. The Ramsden family, for whose estate the pictured buildings were named, features in many place names in and around our town. The Ramsdens acquired the Crown lands here when purchasing them from Elizabeth I in the late 16th century. They made significant contributions to local life that included constructing a waterworks for local domestic use and, in 1761, erected a market cross. The following decade, Sir John Ramsden had a navigable canal built, providing a link with the River Calder and the town centre. Another John Ramsden laid the foundation stone for the Royal Infirmary in 1829 and was an influential member of the Board of Improvement established in 1848. The lands continued in the ownership of the family until 1920 when the Corporation bought them for £1.3 million, thus becoming 'the town that bought itself'. The Estate Buildings were designed by W H Crossland and contain heraldic shields on the first floor that show the Ramsden marriage lines.

Above: Market Place in 1889, shows a fledgling Freeman Hardy and Willis shoe shop on the corner selling 'Single Pairs at Affordable Prices'. Next door is the Patent Office with fine carriages pulled up outside and just after the passage we can see Liptons Irish Butter and Ham Merchants.

Below: It is very interesting to compare these differing views in different decades as they show the changing face of Huddersfield in some aspects but also those familiar places and buildings which have changed very little over time. In this image from 1910 of Market Place in the town centre, not only is the town free of traffic but there are also very few shoppers around; money at this time was very tight indeed for most families. The five chaps are gathered at the corner around a large and ornate gas lamp which compliments the memorial fountain just behind them. Several large ornamental bushes and shrubs enhance the small square.

Right: The bustling area around Market Place looking down John William Street suggests this could be a Saturday afternoon in Huddersfiled.

Below: A higher lever shot of New Street and Market Place shows changes which have taken out the memorial fountain, gas lamps and shrubs and replaced them with a paved area and a newly constructed Huddersfield Borough Police box. The smart cars parked on the left are an indication of traffic growth with more of the general public visiting the town on buses and trams.

Bottom: Looking in the opposite direction, the Police Box remains, traffic lights have appeared and the dominant Burtons Building takes pride of place next to the Refuge Assurance Building, previously the premises of the Waverley Temperance Hotel. Shoppers, traffic and buses have all increased in this late 1930s photo. The edges of pavements outside Rushworth's store on the opposite corner were painted black and white to aid pedestrians, possible due to blackouts in the war years. On the far side of Burtons is the YMCA building which was a central point of meeting for the youth of Huddersfield at the time.

Below: Here we can see the Huddersfield Library under construction by J Wimpenny & Co in June 1938. It was opened two years later on 15 April, 1940, by Mayor Alderman Norman Crossley, with the first book being loaned out to the wife of Alderman Smailes.

Top right: Not a normal street scene we would associate with this period, particularly with the endless auto car washes, drive through car washes and 'by hand' car washes we have around these days. We just hope the boys and the girl in the photo have permission to wash this fine car on a local street. The girl may be from the local brownies or girl guides, earning some coppers to add to a fund; she seems to be doing a good job, standing on those wide running boards. The little boy is cleaning what he can reach and no doubt polishing the badges on a car we can't quite identify sadly. On the pavement, the little chap on the left may have 'lost his marbles' as he is looking closely at the ground or maybe it's the pennies they have been paid for a job well done. It's good to see the pram wheels on the boy's cart had been put to good use. Is he tidying his cart of cloths and soap for their next job?

Did you know?

Evidence of Saxon settlement are indicated by place names that had such endings as Ham, Ley or Ton as well as Burgh, Worth and Stead. Hence Meltham, Honley, Bradley, Dalton, Deighton and Almondbury all indicate Saxon settlement.

Left: Boots has now become a household name in most towns and cities across the UK. From its humble beginnings in 1849 when John Boot opened a herbalist store in Goose Gate Nottingham, it appointed its first chemist in 1884 and was renamed the Boots Pure Drug Company in 1888, probably not a name it would choose these days. The Devonshire Buildings were at the junction of King Street and Victoria Lane, locally known as 'Boots Corner'. A little further along from the corner can be seen one of Montague Burtons Shops – 'The Tailor of Taste' or so it claimed around the time of this photograph was taken in September 1950.

GEORGE

NO ENTRY

Top left and Above: Only smart limousines, please, would seem to be the message for those rolling up outside the George Hotel. After all, there was a reputation to be maintained. Designed by William Wallen and Charles Child, it was built to complement the neighbouring railway station. It is a Grade II listed building that retained its Victorian elegance whilst being kept up to date in its interior comforts. The George has an excellent array of rugby league memorabilia. It was within these walls that the game, particularly popular in the north of England, was formalised. In 1895, the Northern Rugby Union Football broke from the Rugby Union Football organisation. At a meeting held in this hotel on 29 August, representatives of the former group decided, by a vote of 20 to 1, that their members would go it alone and take a step towards professionalism. Dewsbury was the only dissenting voice. Two other clubs joined soon after, swelling the early ranks to 22. At first, the old rugby union laws were used, but these were modified by 1907 to include changes to the number of players in a team, the play the ball rule, no lineouts and two points for all goals successfully kicked. The game's Heritage Centre was opened in the hotel basement on 30 August, 2005, by household names Billy Boston, Neil Fox and Mick Sullivan.

Left: St George's Square 1938. A Scammell motor wagon can be seen in the distance behind the trams and trolley buses. The Belisha Beacon was introduced as one of Leslie Hore-Belisha's, measures to improve road safety during his time as Transport Minister from 1934-1937. He had described the 7,343 deaths on the roads recorded in 1934 as 'mass murder' and introduced the 30mph speed limit for cars in built-up areas as the previous 20mph speed limit had been continually ignored. With a massive increase in vehicle numbers and population today, the 2,337 deaths recorded in 2009 in the UK are still too many, but the Cabinet Minister of 1934 would have been pleased to see the impact of road safety progress.

Did you know?

Huddersfield was the birthplace of Rugby League. On 29 August, 1895, twenty two northern clubs met in the George Hotel to set up their own Northern Rugby Football Union which became the Rugby Football League in 1922.

Above and below: The above view of Westgate in the early 1950s shows little traffic in what now is a busy part of Huddersfield. A trolley bus loading for Waterloo can be seen in the centre with the main meeting points in the photograph being Manor's Corner, Cherry Tree Corner and Rushworth's Corner. The Victorian buildings stand proudly as the main architecture of the time, but with the odd shop front becoming modernised, such as Sharp's Floor Furnishers to the left. Below, looking up Westgate from Rushworth's Corner the traffic is clearly heavier at this point and the pedestrians are having to watch their way their way across the road overseen by the bobby on the right.

Above: Much of Buxton Road was swept away in 1965 as part of a redevelopment scheme. In earlier years it was home to the impressive building that belonged to the Huddersfield Industrial Society. The first form of co-operative society in Huddersfield was established in 1829 and took the form of a combined Co-operative Trading and Manufacturing Association, occupying a shop in Westgate, near the Wellington Hotel. The Industrial Society, a formalised organisation more akin to the Rochdale Pioneers, was founded in 1860 at a meeting at the Albion Hotel. A grocery store was opened on Buxton Road. Before long, a butchery was added and the society soon branched out further, introducing a drapery department. Things went from strength to strength. By the turn of the century, the movement was so successful that these grand premises, designed by J Berry, were opened in 1906. In 1937, the part of the enterprise that housed fish, game, vegetable and fruit sales, amongst other commodities to the right were replaced by a modernist, semi art deco style of building. The long, continuous style of windows seemed at odds with the architecture of its established neighbour. It still does today, but we should be grateful that we still have the handsome clock tower and the Edwardian building below. Buxton Road is now New Street.

Below: Here we see Ramsden Street in 1957 with the Theatre Royal on the left. The theatre was opened in September 1859 but demolished in 1961, together with the buildings opposite, to make way from the new Market Hall.

ENTERTAINMENT LEISURE & PASTIMES

Below: Steady as you go, girls. Hitch up those skirts and take your chances on a ducking. Still, nothing ventured etc and we are happy to report that they made it safely, and dryly, to the other side. Of course, had a dainty toe entered the water there would have been much squealing as befitted young ladies having fun in 1907. The woman to the rear, either their mother or a governess, had more problems as her skirts required more gathering than those of her charges. The stepping stones on the waters at Spa Bottom in Lepton just demanded to be used. All that this group did was go across them and then come straight back again. There was no need to go over. Just the sheer joy of being out in the fresh air and having a little adventure was enough excuse to make the trip. Even as late as Edwardian times, girls were still regarded in middle class circles as being rather delicate flowers. It was thought that they needed adult company whenever out and about as they could not possibly think for themselves or take on some sort of personal responsibility. In a few years' time, as young women, they would be nursing the war wounded, driving ambulances and operating machinery in factories and on the land. There were no chaperones then.

Above: Farnley Tyas was created an urban district in its own right in 1894. It still had this status in 1916 when Mrs W Barrowclough and her children posed for the camera. They were neatly dressed in such a way that would suggest the family was well above the breadline. What is not clear is the effect that the 1914-18 War was having on her and the kiddies. Perhaps her husband at this very moment was up to his knees in some foxhole on the Somme. If so, all she could do was say a prayer and hope that one day Johnny would come marching home. Farnley Tyas is still the quiet village it was a century ago. In a picturesque rural setting, just four miles south of Huddersfield, it sits in an elevated position overlooking a mixture of woodland and fields. The rather quaint name of the settlement possibly comes from a corruption of 'ferns' and 'lea' being combined with that of the Le Teys family of feudal lords.

Right: The boy has presumably been given the job of looking after his sister. He decided that playing at horses and carts was a good way of keeping her happy. She looks to be precariously perched, but children never get anywhere in life without experiencing a few dangers and suffering the odd tumble or grazed knee. Back in 1894, the children were far removed from a world of Nintendos, X-Boxes and computer generated graphics. They had to make their own entertainment and use something that is under exercised by 21st century kiddies; an imagination. The lad would have rushed about whinnying and tossing his head as he pretended to be Black Beauty, the equine hero of Anna Sewell's 1877 novel. Of course, he would either have read the book or had the story told to him at bedtime. Youngsters now would wait until the DVD was issued. When the little girl tired of pretending to be the lady of the manor and put down the imaginary reins, she turned to her dolls' house and spent a happy time rearranging the furniture and talking to her other toys. Life as a child was never dull. There was no time to be bored as there was always some new idea to be explored. Tomorrow, the children could go big game hunting in Africa or drive a stagecoach in the Wild West. All they had to do was use a little bit of imagination. As they say nowadays, easy innit.

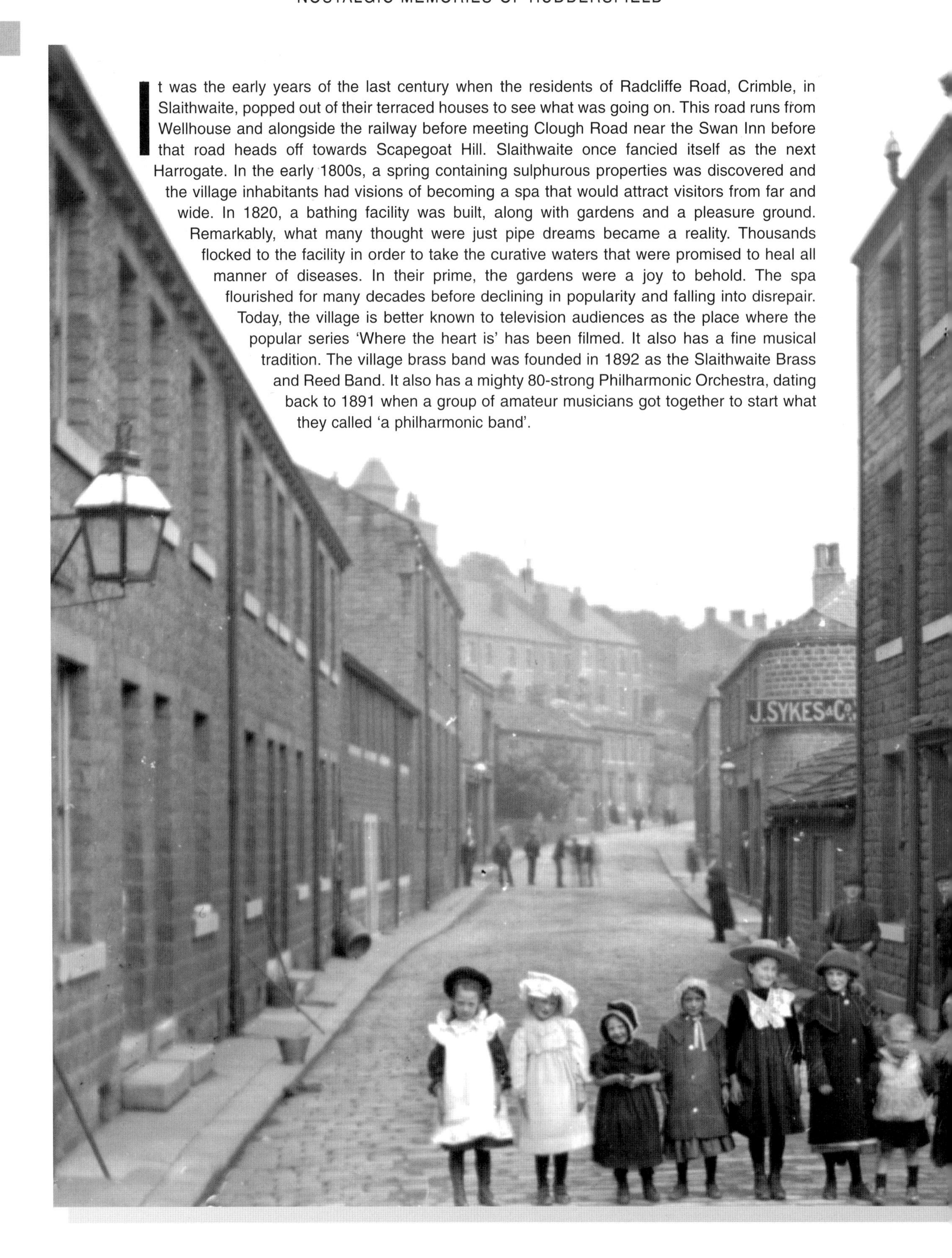

It was the early years of the last century when the residents of Radcliffe Road, Crimble, in Slaithwaite, popped out of their terraced houses to see what was going on. This road runs from Wellhouse and alongside the railway before meeting Clough Road near the Swan Inn before that road heads off towards Scapegoat Hill. Slaithwaite once fancied itself as the next Harrogate. In the early 1800s, a spring containing sulphurous properties was discovered and the village inhabitants had visions of becoming a spa that would attract visitors from far and wide. In 1820, a bathing facility was built, along with gardens and a pleasure ground. Remarkably, what many thought were just pipe dreams became a reality. Thousands flocked to the facility in order to take the curative waters that were promised to heal all manner of diseases. In their prime, the gardens were a joy to behold. The spa flourished for many decades before declining in popularity and falling into disrepair. Today, the village is better known to television audiences as the place where the popular series 'Where the heart is' has been filmed. It also has a fine musical tradition. The village brass band was founded in 1892 as the Slaithwaite Brass and Reed Band. It also has a mighty 80-strong Philharmonic Orchestra, dating back to 1891 when a group of amateur musicians got together to start what they called 'a philharmonic band'.

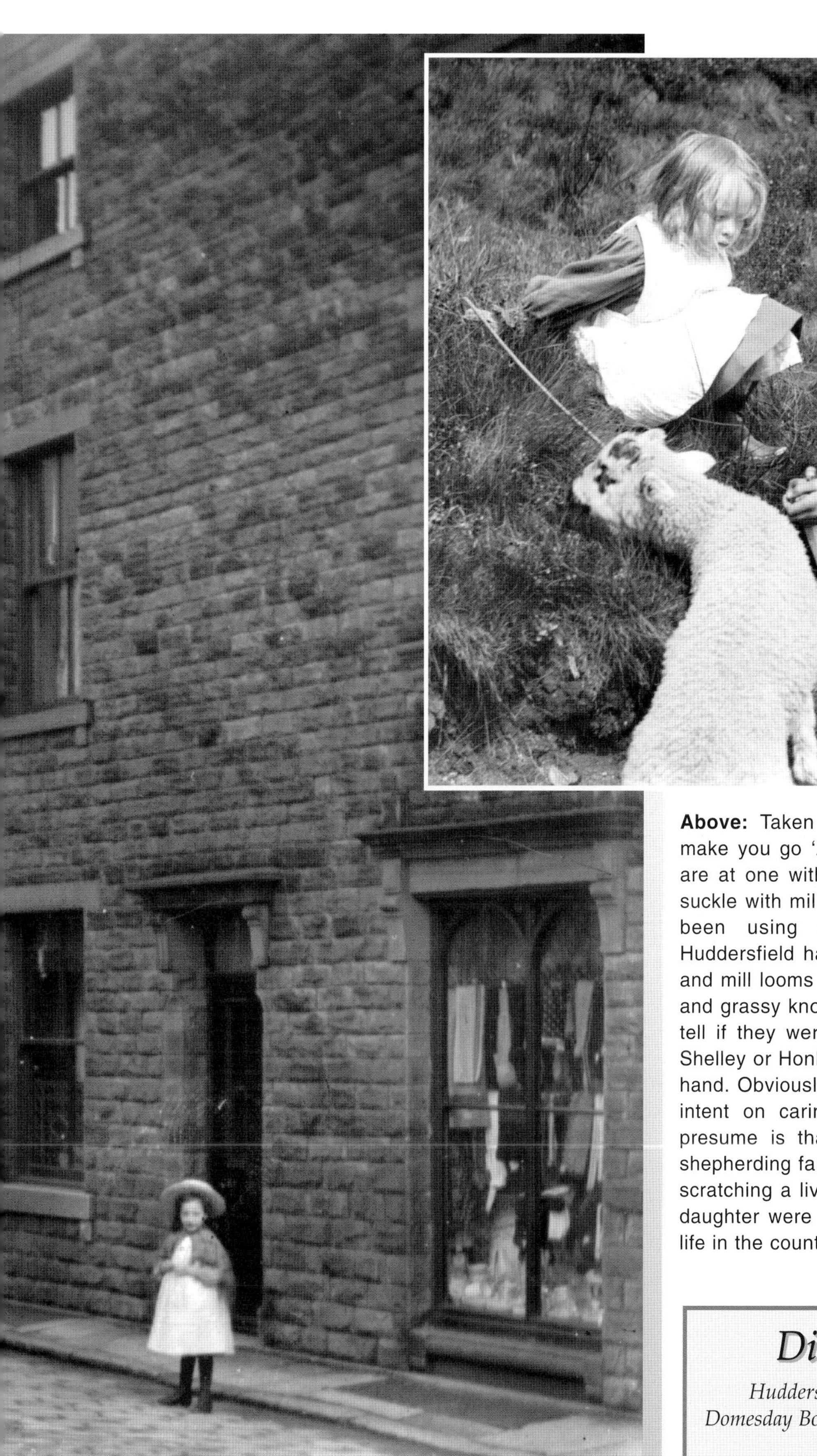

Above: Taken in 1899, this picture is one to make you go 'Aaah'. The mother and daughter are at one with nature as they help the lambs suckle with milk from a bottle that the child had been using only a few months earlier. Huddersfield has not been all factory chimneys and mill looms in its past. There are rolling hills and grassy knolls within easy reach. We cannot tell if they were near Penistone or Greenfield, Shelley or Honley, or even if they were closer to hand. Obviously, they did not care as they were intent on caring for their lambs. All we can presume is that they belong to a farming or shepherding family. Theirs would be a tough lot, scratching a living from the land. Yet, mum and daughter were able to show the gentler side of life in the countryside.

Did you know?

Huddersfield was mentioned in The Domesday Book in 1086 as a village known as Oderesfelt.

Below: The grounds of the vicarage at Almondbury provided the setting for the photograph from 1907. Parts of All Hallows Church date back to the 13th century, but the traditions of the maypole dance go back even further. It is thought to have links with ancient fertility rites and is thus connected with rural settings in places that relied heavily on produce from the land. The children were probably the off-spring of local inhabitants who were employed in woollen factories, working with mohair, sealskin and manufacturing fancy vestings. They would not have been much concerned about the success of the crops and, for them, the maypole dance was just a country tradition that the teachers at school got them to do each year as a treat for the parents. The ribbon dance had become especially popular since the early 18th century, so much so that some variety artists included a form of it in their stage acts. The Almondbury kiddies were not that adept. They were happy enough to get through their routine with only the occasional tangle or collision with the child next to them. Those of us who recall taking part in such dances cannot remember a single occasion when disaster of some form did not strike. It was usually caused by some naughty boy trying to 'liven things up'.

Right: Every village has its own identity and most residents of long standing jealously guard it. In Kirklees, with its many rural outposts, there are dozens of such places. Most of them expressed some objection to becoming part of a metropolitan borough in 1974 as they were very happy just being from plain old Yorkshire. But, this was just one of the changes that seemed to take them that little bit further away from being villagers and transforming them into townies. As commuting became the thing for workers, then the small settlements just outside towns and cities became popular places to set up home. The 'incomers' often had few ties with tradition and only some of them tried to blend in and adopt the ways that successive generations of

locals had established. Even a small village like Kirkheaton held its own carnival each year. The children on this float from c1910 looked towards the camera with a mixture of expressions. There seems to have been something of a gender divide. The girls appear to be quite happy in their costumes, whereas the lads generally have glum faces, suggesting that their mums had to indulge in a mixture of threat and cajoling to get them dressed and into place. This float was sponsored by George Mallinson and Sons, a local manufacturing chemist. Based at Gawthorp Green, opposite the old riding stables, this was a considerable enterprise. The premises comprised an extensive warehouse, with sheds, laboratory, counting house and offices. The manufacturing portion of the site was fitted out with a full complement of all the requisite appliances and general plant.

Right: A Huddersfield giant amongst the soft drinks world of Britain and Europe, Benjamin Shaw & Sons was a major employer in the town, expanding to Oldham in 1964. It was founded in 1871 and opened a factory in Willow Lane in 1894. It was the first company to put a fizzy drink in a can and many will remember the Suncharm brand exported all over the world. The children here are enjoying Ben Shaw's pop from this stall at the ICI Children's Gala in 1958. The boy near the back of the queue, in his school blazer, is waiting expectantly for the three sales ladies, all smiling, to help the children in front and hoping there is some pop left for him.

Above: It was a natural behaviour of the time that neighbours looked out for each other and families played and socialised together. They also had gala days in their neighbourhood and this one at Lindley Carnival was a good example. Held in June 1953, it looks a pretty cold day considering the overcoats, macs and scarves being worn. But this didn't stop the children having a great time, with beaming smiles whilst on their train ride. The little boy at the front looks to be in his element and possible had aspirations of becoming a train driver and who knows, he may have even become one.

Bottom left: Zebras and giraffes would always excite children's imagination particularly if they were part of a fairground roundabout ride. These children are enjoying a family day out at the Hopkinsons Ltd Children's Gala in July 1959 and are very smartly dressed in their 'Sunday best'. The public announcements van in the background was probably loaned by Exide Batteries and will have played an important role in the day, making sure that contestants were at the races and competitions on time and lost children were quickly re-united with their parents. The roundabout ride would have been a manual affair and the lady in the pretty floral dress in the foreground looks to be lending a helping band for her son in the galleon type seat.

Below: It was a time for cooling down and having fun at Greenhead park paddling pool in this photo of the mid-1950s. The park was expanded over many years and this pool was added in 1934. It may have sown the seeds for young children to get more into swimming and follow a future Olympic star such as Huddersfield's own Anita Lonsbrough. The little boy in the foreground is already practising his font crawl stroke in complete safety, whilst parents watch from their seats at the side.

Did you know?

Anita Lonsbrough from Huddersfield, won gold in the 200m breaststroke in 2:49s at the 1960 Summer Olympics in Rome, on 27 August, 1960, at the age of 19, setting a new world record time. She would also be the last British woman to win Olympic gold in swimming until Rebecca Adlington did so in the 2008 Summer Olympics, 48 years later.

Left: Although television was emerging as a form of entertainment for the family, there were still very few television sets in the home at the time of this picture, taken in December 1953. Huddersfield was still a stronghold for cinemagoers with over 25 separate cinemas in the Huddersfield area. The Empire Cinema, shown here, was screening the film, 'Code of the Secret Service' a 1939 film starring none other than Ronald Reagan. What irony that he should become the leader of the most powerful nation on earth in January 1981.

Below: The Majestic Cinema in Viaduct Street was probably less majestic than other cinemas around, as this shot from 1962 shows, but it still catered for the varying tastes of cinemagoers. Showing at this time was the popular John Wayne film, The Comancheros, a 1961 'Deluxe CinemaScope colour film' which also starred Lee Marvin. The area around Viaduct Street looks pretty quiet at the time and even the Regent Garage opposite is not seeing much trade.

Above: This photo shows the 1974 conversion of the ABC Cinema on Market Street from one large 2,000 seat cinema into two smaller ones, becoming Huddersfield's first multi-screen cinema. The new premises were completed in February 1974. It is clear to see what's on, the X rated 'Enter the Dragon' a 1973 Hong Kong martial arts film starring Bruce Lee who sadly died shortly after making the film in July of that year. The film also starred Jackie Chan who has risen to much greater fame in recent times. Paper Moon was on screen two, another 1973 film starring Ryan and Tatum O'Neal, transferring their real-life father and daughter relationship to the big screen as Moses and Addie. It would be interesting to know which film the girl in the doorway will be going to see, as long as her boyfriend turns up in time.

Did you know?

James Mason the legendary film actor was. born, James Neville Mason on 15 May 1909 in Huddersfield. During his film career he was nominated for three Academy Awards.

Patrick Stewart, famous for is his role as Captain Jean-Luc Picard in Star Trek, was born July 13, 1940 in Mirfield near Huddersfield. He is currently Chancellor of the University of Huddersfield.

Left: As part of the conversion of the ABC Cinema in Market Street in 1974, the projection room also had an update. The technician can be seen splicing the various films and advertisements for the evening's entertainment, which then fed onto 'the cake stand' as the apparatus below him was known. The evening could then run uninterrupted, as long as the splicings held, and the audience would be blissfully unaware that a single technician had helped them enjoy their evening out.

Left: Jive was definitely on its way in as a new dance craze, as can be seen by the couple in the foreground of this shot. They seem to be leading the room towards a more energetic form of dance. Although others seemed happy with their more sedate and intimate waltz style of dancing. It was 1956 at the ICI Works Ball, where the ladies wore satin and taffeta and blazers seemed to be popular for the gents. It was clearly a popular event and everyone

was on the dance floor. Imperial Chemical Industries was once one of Huddersfield's biggest employers, employing thousands at the Leeds Road chemical works. This type of events was a great opportunity for employees to 'let down their hair' and an opportunity for the company to show its appreciation to the hard-working staff.

Above: A deserved winner no doubt as this little girl stands in front of the lady judges of the fancy dress competition at an ICI Children's Gala Day in June 1959. And you've guessed it, she is 'The little old woman who lived in a shoe'. The large crowds are enjoying a sunny day and many seem to be enthralled by the fancy dress event.

Left: A great race by the mum's of the day, shoes off and get on with it. Today would probably require matching Lycra shorts and tops with high spec trainers and wrist bands plus a 20-minute warm up. The race was held at the ICI Children's Gala Day in June 1957 and it's great to see so many taking part. It seemed a key event of the day if we judge by the crowd gathered around and cheering the mums along. It's a clear win for the lady in the foreground as she 'bursts' through the finishing (or is it washing) line. Maybe she was emulating 'the flying housewife', Fanny Blanker-Keon, a nickname she earned after the London Olympics in 1948. The dutch athlete championed women's athletics as a 30-year-old mother of two, winning four gold medals.

ROYAL VISITS

Right: Built in 1864, Wellington Mills in Lindley had the distinction of a Royal visit by King George V and Queen Mary in 1912. The growing textile company was Huddersfields largest employer in the cloth trade with over 1,400 employees.

Below: A return visit was made by King George V and Queen Mary to Wellington Mills in Lindley in the 1930s. The crowds were certainly larger than appeared in 1912 and all were cheering and waving their St George flags as the Royal motorcade arrives.

Below: The ladies and gentlemen dressed in top hat and tails and summer gowns, seem to be a little concerned as they are looking around anxiuosly for someone to appear. This image of a visiting party of Royals to Holmfirth in 1927 who were cleary lucky with the weather for the day, shows the group in 'nervous anticipation'.

Below: A mass of people and marching soldiers were at Greenhead Park in 1912 to welcome King George V and Queen Mary. Only a few minutes earlier this scene looked orderly and calm with a clear roadway through the centre. Straw boaters were the headgear of choice for the men on these occasions and summer bonnets for the ladies, in their long skirts and fashionable blouses the scene would make a great spectacle for the royals in one of Huddersfield's great parks

enjoying the day and thankfully there will be little thought of anything sinister from a security point of view. The street was decorated with bunting and flags and the crowds had been waiting for up to four hours according to local press reports from the time.

Left: Here we have the police escort on the new Triumph Twin motorcycle, prompting the crowds to stand back as the royal motorcade arrives. We are informed that the motorcycle was brand new that day and therefore it was on royal duty from the start. It was considered the most influential bike of its day and could reach 85mph from its 489cc engine which provided 25bhp. The children appear much more interested in the photographer and the imminent arrival of the royal couple. However, the little boy with his mother just beyond the police escort does seem to be checking out the new offering from Triumph.

Left: A smiling Princess Elizabeth can be seen here in the motorcade on her visit to Huddersfield in July 1949. It is a charming shot and shows the present Queen in a wide brimmed hat with the dress being described as taffeta in lime green and white with small checks. The dress was full skirted with three quarter length sleeves and a pleated neckline. This shot was taken she left Learoyd's Mill. Unfortunately, Prince Phillip, seated next to Princess Elizabeth, is obscured by the wide brim of the natural straw hat which completes the outfit.

Below: The royal motorcade is shown here moving slowly along New Street and flanked by police horses for protection, but only form the enthusiastic crowds. The couple in an open topped Daimler are

Above: These people were enjoying the sunshine whilst waiting for the Princess Elizabeth and the Duke of Edinburgh to appear. They are outside the Huddersfield Town Hall. The royal couple had been visiting Trafalgar Mills owned by Learoyd Brothers. The firm was founded in the late 19th Century by Mr. A. E. Learoyd and his brother Mr. Frank Learoyd. Learoyd's had established a superlative reputation for their fine worsteds and their products were sought after by buyers throughout the world. The royal couple would then go on to see over 8,000 school children perform at Leeds Road sports ground.

Right: Princess Alexandra can be seen in the Mayor's Reception Room, Huddersfield Town Hall. She was born on Christmas Day in 1936, (Alexandra Helen Elizabeth Olga Christabel) and was the youngest daughter of King George V. She is, at the time of writing, 39th in line of succession to the throne and among her many patronages she is Patron of the Guide Dogs for the Blind Association and of Action for Blind People as well as being President of Sight Savers International.

that week to gain such an important position. A beautiful day meant that everyone waited patiently and waved their flags in the sunshine.

Left: Princess Margaret is dressed in black following the death of Queen Mary. The Princess was visiting Huddersfield Parish Church in April 1953 for morning service at the invitation of her friend the Rev Phips. The Princess would visit again in 1958 to open the new girls' school.

Below: The new sports centre in Huddersfield was opened on 24 November, 1973, by Princess Anne. The building, which cost £900,000 at the time was an important step forward for the town in providing modern up-to-date training and sports facilities for the people of Huddersfield. The two swimming pools would provide great opportunities for children wishing to follow in the footsteps, or should it be the wake, of Anita Lonsbrough, Huddersfield's own Olympic champion. The Princess, see here talking to one of the gymnasts, was presented with honorary family membership by the mayor, however we cannot find any evidence of any of the royals taking up that membership.

Bottom left: The children from Waverley School, Edgerton Road, are immaculately turned out in their smart school uniforms. They are excitedly awaiting the arrival of Princess Elizabeth and Prince Phillip on their royal visit in 1949. The little girls look almost angelic, holding their posies of flowers, whilst the little boys on the front row must have been very well behaved

WARTIME

Above: They marched out in the late summer of 1914, vowing to be back by Christmas. Some did not last more than a day or two on the battlefield. The horrors of war in the trenches only gradually filtered back home as telegram after telegram was brought to the front door where wives, sweethearts and mothers received the news that their loved ones were not returning. Information from the front was censored and letters home only spoke in guarded terms about what was being endured. When the wounded were repatriated it became obvious that it was not just the dead who were casualties. There were some men who were so badly injured, either physically or mentally, that they would never return to normality. This group of soldiers includes some with lower limb injuries. Perhaps they were suffering from trench foot, caused by standing for hours in waterlogged trenches with no chance to change out of sodden socks and boots. If untreated, the infected areas could turn gangrenous and require amputation. In that first winter of the war, some 20,000 soldiers had to receive treatment. The 12-bedded Holmfirth Military Cottage Hospital opened in 1914 and evolved into the 60 bed Holmfirth Auxiliary Hospital during the war. It was later replaced by the Memorial Hospital. The nursing staff was kind and comforting and it broke some of the nurses' hearts to see a number of the brave men in their charge laid so low.

Top right: This group, enjoying a quiet drink by the tea bar, includes the flower of England's young manhood who went optimistically off to battle in 1914. They were ill prepared for what the enemy hurled at them. Many joined up for what they thought was going to be a jolly adventure, with just a hint of danger. The reality

was something else. A large number, especially those from the north of England, enlisted in Pals' battalions. These were made up of men from the same part of a town or those from factory floors who worked together. One of the leading army generals, Henry Rawlinson, was a keen supporter of the Pals, believing that men would more readily enlist if they had a friend or neighbour doing the same. The result was that when such a battalion suffered heavy casualties, the devastating effect on a local neighbourhood was out of all proportion to others. The soldier second from the right has been identified as Walter Smith from Almondbury.

Below: Trolley buses were not just for transporting the public, they played a key role in advertising for the war effort between 1939 and 1945. This trolley bus can bee seen in St George's Square during National Service Week, promoting recruitment into the various armed services. The slogans on the bus read, 'Civil Defence is Your Business' and 'National Service- Offer Yourself Today'. There is also a banner on the side for the Dukes 7th Battalion which was based in Huddersfield.

Below: Father Christmas had arrived at Kaye's drapery store on King Street. According to the company slogan, this was 'the place for smart drapers'. Children were not that bothered about reputations and cloth dealing, but they did take an interest in the grand old man in a red suit, with a face adorned with white whiskers. For a modest tanner (the old sixpence) they got to visit his grotto and receive a present from the wishing well. They were not that bothered that he seemed to have lost several stone and was six inches shorter than when they saw him at school the week before. Christmas was a magical time when all things were possible, even dramatic changes in physique. They knew that there was a war on. The grown-ups kept saying so. But, for a short while, they could forget all about Hitler and his cronies. Kaye's window displays often had messages of encouragement to local people for them to contribute to the war effort. On this occasion, women were being urged to join the services or to do their bit in nursing or the civil defence. People were also asked to contribute to government coffers by buying national savings certificates or war bonds. By 1943, some £5 million worth of certificates had been issued. Some older readers might recall getting shiny red and blue badges to mark special purchases. They had the slogan 'Lend to defend' printed on them.

Right: Here we see yet another impact of the war on Huddersfield life, particularly that of the ladies of Huddersfield. The photo of the tram was taken in 1940 and shows the first conductresses who were brought in to replace the men who had been called up to enlist in the war. Brought in, was the operative phrase here as many were ordered in to work by being offered the options of a job in munitions or transport. If they chose transport they could expect to become 'clippies' on the trams, some ladies did become drivers, but very few. You may remember, the 'clippies' with their leather bags for change and coin holders for silver. They could expect Sundays off but would have to work through the week and a busy Saturday

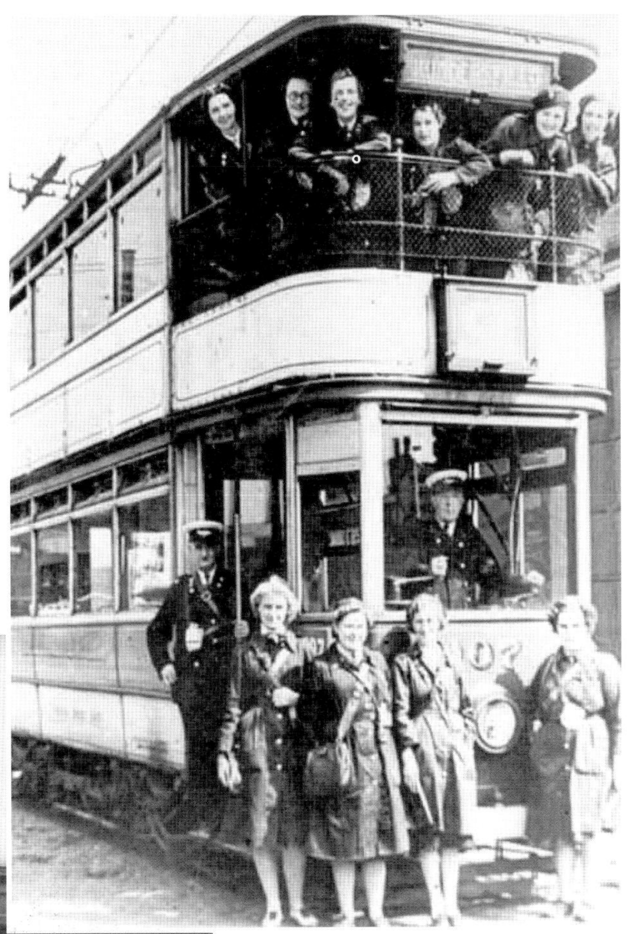

night, taking the fares, looking after passengers and flipping the seats back at a terminus before the return journey. In many cases the 'clippies' were provided with 'ten bob' of change, which doesn't seem much these days at just fifty pence, but if they forgot this for their work that day they could be fined a whole shilling. But they all seem happy enough in this photo of the Huddersfield tram number 107.

Below: During World War II, the general public got used to messages from government and civil defence sources that were wrapped up in catchy phrases. 'Put that light out' was favoured during the blackout. 'Be like dad, keep mum' and 'Careless talk costs lives' warned us that spies might be listening. 'Dig for victory' and 'Lend a hand on the land' urged us to help with food production. 'Make do and mend' was another famous phrase that was aimed at every housewife in the country. In June 1941, clothing rationing was introduced. Just 66 coupons were issued annually, only enough for one outfit. Women were encouraged to repair and remake their family's old clothes. Curtains were cut up to make skirts and dresses and unwanted jumpers were unravelled and knitted into something else. Alfred Kaye's drapery shop had a variety of patriotic messages on display in the summer of 1944. The week before had been given over to a national 'Salute the Soldier' fund-raising campaign. Kaye's decided to follow this up with its own 'Salute the Home Worker' week. The shop window Make Do and Mend display showed what could be done with old garments. This included 'Stop Press – take out your zips and press studs' and 'Look out for that tear and make a dinky repair'.

Above: The parade ground of St Paul's Street Drill Hall was the place for detailed preparation for the Guard of Honour to be presented to the Duke of Edinburgh later that day. It would be a proud day for all involved and everything must be to military precision and perfect presentation of uniform and flags. The children look on in the background to make sure everything is just right. It's unlikely that the truck at the back, labelled Scarborough would be involved given its dusty condition and could have been simply a practical transport vehicle.

Top right: A great day for the people of the town who gathered on a sunny Tuesday in 1949 to witness the Duke of Edinburgh inspecting the Guard of Honour outside the Huddersfield Town Hall in Ramsden Street. The Guard of Honour was made up of the 5th and 7th Battalions of the Duke of Wellington's Regiment and the 538 LAA Regiment RA. The Duke spoke with Colour Sergeant George Radcliffe, of Slaithwaite, and Lance Bombardier Herbert Baker, of Sheepbridge, possibly about the medals adorning their uniforms or how their veteran friends were doing. The Huddersfield and District Cricket League had sent a special telegram to the Duke and Princess Elizabeth that day, extending their 'loyal greetings' from their 10,000 members. Herbert Robinson, President of the Cricket League received a telegram of thanks for the 'kind message' from Prince Philip.

Right: The pile of sandbags around the base of the Library and Art Gallery on what is now called Princess Alexandra Walk place the date of this photograph as 1940. It was the year in which German planes began to fly regular bombing missions, attacking our towns and cities in what became known as 'the blitz'. They mainly targeted those that had industrial significance or could contribute to the war effort, but the enemy was not averse to attacking the cultural heart of Britain as well. Civil defence groups worked hard in trying to protect people and property, but in truth there was little one could do to

guard against 500 lbs of explosive falling directly upon a single place. The Library building dates from the 1930s, so it was still fairly new when war broke out. The walkway on which it stands was named for the woman who was the only daughter of the Duke of Kent, the fourth son of King George V. Alexandra lost her father in a plane crash when she was only five. Her mother, Princess Marina, never remarried. Alexandra was one of the bridesmaids when her cousin, the future Elizabeth II, married Prince Philip in 1947. She married Angus Ogilvy in 1963. The ceremony at Westminster Abbey was televised and watched by an estimated audience of 200 million across the world. She was widowed in 2004.

SHOPPING SPREE

Above: How many married couples out there went to Fillans to get those precious love tokens that they have worn with a mixture of affection and pride ever since? When the young beau popped the question it was the start of what he hoped would be a long journey. The first step towards sealing that commitment came with the purchase of the engagement ring. That was a difficult one to take, because the future bride and groom often bought it together. He did not want to appear too mean and she did not wish to be thought of as a pushy gold-digger. That was where the diplomacy of the jeweller entered the arena. His experienced eye summed up the situation and guided them both to stones and settings that were attractive and seemed to be in the right price range. Fillans is a family firm that has been in business for over 150 years since opening in 1852. The workforce at the start of the last century, seen outside the shop at 2 Market Walk, included polishers, stone-setters, engravers and other craftsmen in addition to the counter staff. The firm did not just deal in rings, but in all manner of jewellery from watches to bracelets and from pendants to necklaces, using a variety of precious metals. Fillans moved to Market Place in the 1970s and opened another outlet on Stonegate in York during the last decade. There have now been five generations of the family involved in the business, but they have lost count of the number of starry eyed lovers who have passed across their threshold.

Top right: The Corporation acquired market rights in 1876 and set about establishing a competition to design a hall on the site of the butchers' shambles that was in existence at the time. There was keen interest shown, as we can tell from the fact that 30 entries were submitted. Adjudication was made in 1877 and George Edmund Street was declared to have provided the winning design. He was a prominent figure, especially in church architecture. Despite that, the Markets and Fairs Committee rejected the recommendation and turned to locally based Edward Hughes instead. He had been a pupil of the eminent George Gilbert Scott. The Market Hall he conceived opened on King Street on 31 March 1880. The Marks & Spencer stall is a reminder of the humble beginnings of that famous store,

Michael Marks, a Russian Jew, fled from persecution in his homeland and made his new home in England in the early 1880s. He found employment in Leeds and set up his own market stall there in 1884. He married in 1886 and moved with his family to Cheetham Hill, Manchester in 1893. He went into partnership with Thomas Spencer the following year, opening their very first shop. By 1901, the business had grown considerably and they were able to build their own warehouse at Derby Street that became their first registered address and official head quarters. By 1903, their original £600 investment had turned into £30,000.

Below: Elegant shoes indeed, to quote from the plate above the footwear shop. The Shaw & Hallas company was formed when John Shaw and J Elliot Hallas combined forces in 1914 on Westgate. Buttoned boots, brogues and clogs would have been included in lines that would later add stilettos, winkle pickers and Cuban heels to the stock. Many of the goods on display here were handmade, just as clothing was often made to measure. John Shaw started as a shoemaker and repairer when he established a small business in 1864. His wife, a former milliner, helped out and soon there was a family connection with the Halllases, owners of a Holmfirth shoe shop. John's daughter married Elliot Hallas's son and the family links were completed when the two sets of parents joined up their business interests. By the time that this double fronted shop was in use, the respective founders' sons, Jack Shaw and George Hallas, were in charge. The firm moved to John William Street in 1923, about the time that a third generation in shoemaking was represented by Douglas Shaw. By the time Michael Shaw, the great grandson of one of the founders, joined in 1958 the company had abandoned shoe manufacture and was concentrating on retailing. Shaw & Hallas moved to Market Street in 1961 and continues to make sure that locals are well shod from its outlet on Market Walk.

Above: The major building on the left of the picture is Taylor and Hobson Ltd, a prestigious furniture maker which started business in 1899 and continued until 1991. Their history goes back much further and has links with Thomas Chippendale, cabinet maker of Otley. The No.10 Tram can be seen travelling along New Street which seems pretty quiet at this time. The young lad in short trousers crosses the street and appears to be watching the man in the straw boater striding along the pavement on the other side.

Bottom left: The open market on Brook Street was popular with many Huddersfield shoppers as we can see here in the early 1960s. The grand building of the covered market just behind remains a central part of the town's shopping scene today. The Grade II listed building has a magnificent Victorian iron and glass roof canopy and was built between 1887-1889. It was sadly a duller spectacle in the days of this photo, compared to today's fully restored and tastefully painted version. This would not deter the shoppers however, who could buy most things from fabrics to footwear along with their fresh groceries and household items at a price which would not stretch their purse strings too much. A few of the ladies, laden with bags, would no doubt be heading for the trolley bus to take them home or they may be stopping off in one of the small cafes situated under the glass canopy, for a well earned 'cuppa'.

Below: In the early 1930s the wood timber frames of some town centre buildings were still evident and can be seen here above Dunn & Co, hat makers and tailors and the Stylo shoe shop. The No.4 trams from Marsden to Bradley had the added benefit of a small post box on the front which allowed passengers to post their mail at tram stops for a small fee, of course. The image depicts changing times with older trams passing by more recent buildings such as Marks & Spencer on the right.

NO ENTRY
ONE WAY STREET
TAILORING
MAYPOLE

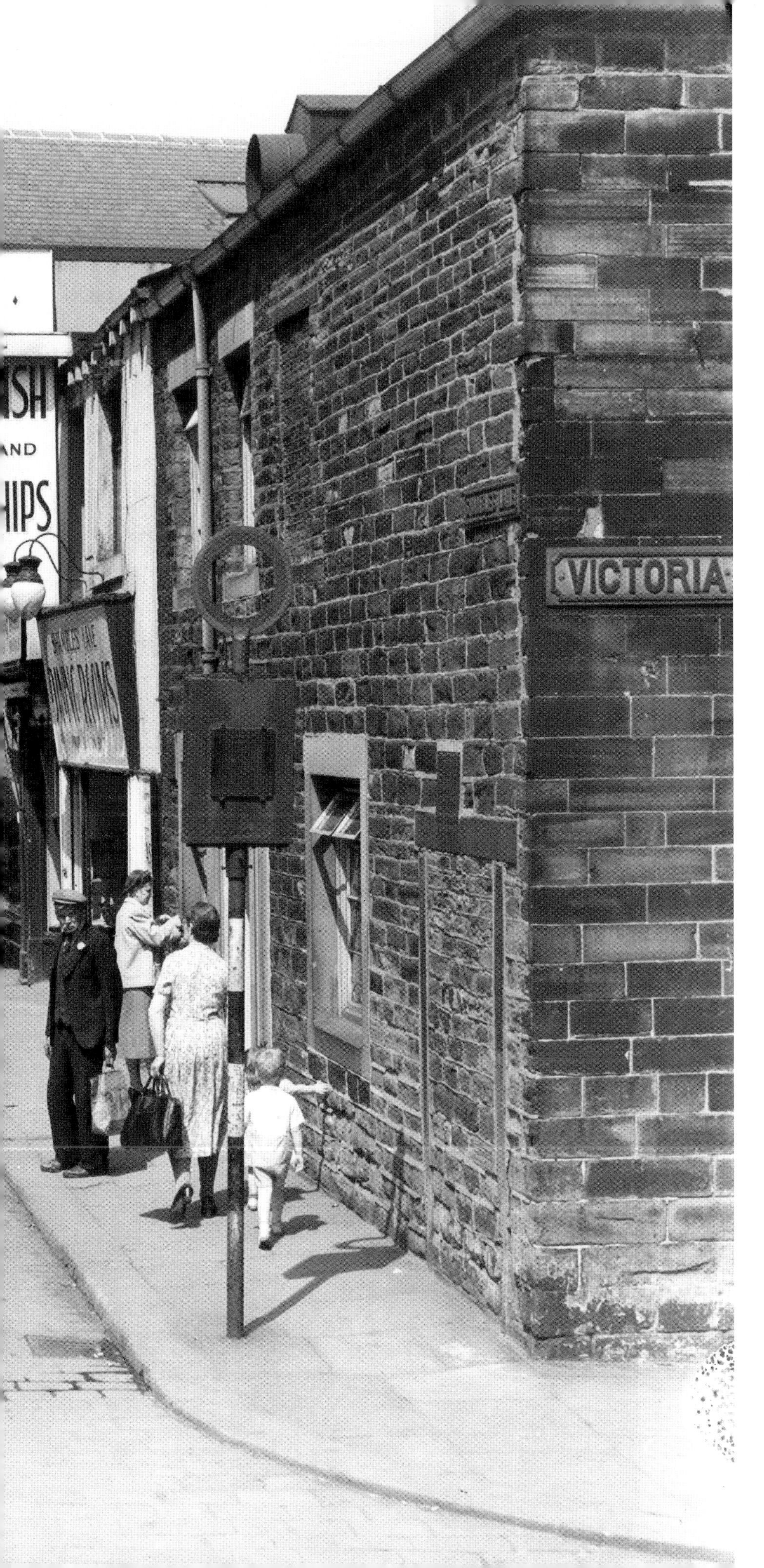

The old Shambles was a busy little cut through from Victoria Street to King Street and across to the Maypole. At one time you would pass Lodge's grocers, Lindon Smith's greengrocers and Taylor's chemists. There was often a lovely aroma coming from the nearby Home and Colonial Tea Store, a company founded in London in 1883 that grew to become a chain of retail outlets. Others preferred to use their sense of taste and popped into the Bull and Mouth for a quick half before passing the shopkeepers' wares in the pavement displays. In this 1950s' scene, the television shop on the right, just beyond the 'chippie', was something of a modern touch on this traditional street. At the start of the decade, there were very few of us who bothered with or could afford a TV. We listened to the radio for our home entertainment and enjoyed 'The Archers', 'ITMA', 'Journey into space' and 'The Goon Show'. It was the Queen's coronation in 1953 that gave the BBC a big boost and the electronics industry a shot in the arm. It was broadcast live to the nation and, within a short time, the nation was hooked on this new media. By the end of the decade, the television set was a standard piece of furniture and aerials sprouted on rooftops across the land.

Above: An early turn-of-the-century image of King Street looking across at Tylers Booksellers on the left. A mix of shoppers are passing what looks like Arthur Tabrum's shop on the right. A lady in a woollen shawl and a little boy with lace collar who must surely be going to somewhere important, perhaps a school choir or party?

Right and facing page: Here we have two 1950s views of King Street showing the east and west perspectives. Both shots show the Market Hall and its impressive clock tower, which will no doubt bring back memories for many. There was great controversy in the town when it was proposed the Market Hall be demolished. However the modernisers won through and the building was finally closed on 28 March, 1970, and subsequently demolished. It was not without tragedy as the tower collapsed during demolition killing two people.

MARKET
HALL
CAFE

Above: Fifty Shilling Tailors was a popular men's and women's outfitter shown here on the corner of Cloth Hall Street. It later changed to John Colliers in the early 1960s. If John Colliers was 'the window to watch' then March could claim ' March the Tailors dress you well' in the advertising campaigns of the time. The shop closest to us is John Hawkins and Sons, a general haberdashery, selling pinafores, tablecloths and other household items. It is intriguing to consider what could be so interesting to have drawn such a crowd to a shop like this, but clearly something has caught the woman's attention.

Bottom left: Cooked chicken was not quite a fast food in May 1961 but it was becoming more available and popular. Shoppers on the corner of Victoria Street would find Winns poultry shop with its Rotis-o-Mat. The little boy in the centre of the picture has found a manhole cover to stand quietly over whilst his mother possibly shops for some of the exotic fish Winns also stocked including shark. The corner edged on to the shambles which can be just seen at the bottom right of the shot.

Below: We have special weeks for this, that and the other and during the last war there were those dedicated to Spitfires, warships and tanks. In 1951, Woods' fishmongers decided to draw upon that idea and have a promotional week devoted to herrings. The delights of the humble fish were explained to this housewife, in front of a slogan that read 'herrings for health'. The stallholder was ahead of his time because it is only latterly that nutritionists have been recommending that oily fish be included in our diet. Herring, mackerel, trout etc are richer in Omega 3 fatty acids than white fish. Having a regular supply of these foods to eat is supposed to be beneficial for our memory cells, if only we could remember where we put the recipé book! Back when Mr Wood was doing the filleting, it was quite popular to have Friday reserved as a day for fish. Catholics abstained from meat on that day as a token linking them with times when people would perform a penance for their sins or would concentrate on spiritual rather than temporal matters. The Friday fish fry was adopted by a lot of non Catholics as well, becoming a traditional custom in many quarters. It was also a good excuse to nip down to the local chippie and enjoy a completely unhealthy but tasty treat. You could even read last week's news in the wrapping paper at the same time.

Above: New Street in 1953 was a hive of activity, with many leading stores located there. Woolworths, a national institution now sadly gone, can be seen at the centre of the picture. Stylo and Timpson's, ever present shoe shops of the era, stood side by side separated only by the alley way to The Albert. Collinsons Café can be seen just before the timbered building on the right. The shoppers were out in numbers as was the traffic but it all paints a scene so typical of the time in a town which was one of Britain's largest.

Below: The woman having a quiet fag in the foreground in 1978 would be tarred and feathered and run out of town these days for committing such a crime. It was a busy morning in the Packhorse Shopping Centre as people made their way from the Kirkgate end towards the distant King Street entrance. Some did not stop to visit any of the shops, using the covered area as a convenient cut through to other parts of town. The name of the centre is a reminder of the days when goods would be transported across difficult terrain where there were no roads that could be accessed by horses pulling carts. Special bridges with low parapets were built so that the panniers on the horses would not snag as they passed. Pack Horse Yard was originally used for stabling for up to 100 animals for the inn that once stood here. The area was cleared in the late 1960s and early 1970s as part of a redevelopment programme.

Right: Rummaging around in the open market on Brook Street, these housewives were after a Monday bargain. They carefully examined the goods on display on each stall and debated whether or not they could get something a few coppers cheaper further along. Yorkshire folk do not part with their hard earned brass all that easily. Value for money, if you please. Much of the market is housed beneath a Victorian canopy in the very heart of the town centre. It was designed by a Borough Surveyor, RS Dugdale, in the late 1890s. The variety of items on sale attracts shoppers who prefer an olde worlde style of purchasing. The plastic wrapped commodities to be found in supermarkets and chain stores are much less attractive. Unfortunately, in the ways of the 21st century, there are fewer opportunities to avoid the curse of pre-packaging, so it is grand when the chance to avoid it comes along. It is also pleasant to exchange a few cheery words with a stallholder. The personal touch has been lost in the pile 'em high sell 'em cheap economy. Now then, luv, how much will you take for this blanket?

Below: Oh great. Just what we want on a Saturday afternoon as we try to do our shopping at the Shambles. In 1978 it was kids whipping past on bikes and now it is those on skateboards or roller blades that create the problem. No, we are not grumpy old people, just ones who like to amble along a pedestrianised area in safety. The Shambles links the Piazza with King Street and was created during the redevelopment of the town centre in the early 1970s. In medieval times the word 'shambles' referred to a slaughterhouse and was gradually adapted to refer to any place where meat was prepared. The old Shambles here was one of the sites from which market traders operated and there were also shops on either side of the row. It was therefore fitting that quite a few of these belonged to butchers who used impressive displays of meat and poultry hanging outside their premises to attract custom. The last open market held here took place in 1876 before moving to a temporary home in the Cloth Hall. The nearby Victorian Market Hall used to add to the ambience of the area, but this was demolished in 1970.

EVENTS & OCCASIONS

Below: During the First World War people had become used to sticking their hands in their pockets and contributing to various drives for the war effort. There were tank weeks, warship collections, bond sales and so on. Contributing cash to a cause became a regular occurrence. The fund raising drive for charity was being carried out on King Street, near George Hall's department store, in 1923. The need to fund munitions and armaments had gone, but there were always other causes that asked for support. The department store was once an individual business with a different name in every town. We now see the same ones wherever we go and when visiting a chain store in a modern shopping mall, not only can you forget which centre you are in, but almost which town you are visiting. They all seem the same. King Street still has its shops, but is now largely pedestrianised. It also provides an entrance to Kingsgate, the modern face of retail with its covered areas and parking facilities.

Top right: Great-grandma was not always the old battleaxe we thought she was. She may have got crotchety in her old age, but she was once the flapper era's equivalent of a dolly bird. She had a sense of fun that went hand in hand with a determination to help those less well off than herself. In July 1928, Muriel Burgess, Hilda Leech, Elsie Harding, Nellie Singleton and Hettie Marshall cast off all inhibitions, replacing them with a variety of costumes as they indulged in a spot of fund raising. No redblooded male could ignore such pretty lasses and soon those collection tins would have been rattling merrily. What evocative first names they had, firmly placing them on a timeline. One day we will do the same for Kylie, Harper, Kayleigh, Jordan and the rest. This jolly quintet was quite representative of young women during this era. The days of subservience to the wishes of men had been challenged by the suffragettes. Taking on traditional male roles during the 1914-18 War by working on heavy machinery, driving lorries and just generally stepping out from behind the kitchen sink had furthered the cause. Women also rebelled against other society restraints and began wearing short skirts and cropping their hair. They took to smoking and going out with lads unchaperoned. Goodness, in the very week that this photograph was taken outside Kaye's and Peters' drapery store, women even got equal voting rights with men for the first time.

Below right: Huddersfield Town was a major force in soccer in the 1920s. The club only entered the Football League in 1910, but nearly went out of business just after the First World War. Locals rallied round and contributed cash to stave off the threat of a merger with Leeds. The fans were quickly rewarded as Town reached the 1920 FA Cup Final and gained promotion to the First Division in the same year. The side lifted the FA Cup in 1922 at Stamford Bridge, thanks to a penalty scored by Billy Smith. This was to be the last occasion that the final was played at a ground other than Wembley, until the temporary move to the Millennium Stadium in 2001. Many of the players involved in the successful run in the 1920s are seen here, either enjoying a day out in a charabanc or possibly on the way to play in a match. This was a popular mode of travel before enclosed coaches became the norm. Many of the "charrers", as they were known, were little more than converted wartime trucks. The Terriers went on to win the Division One title in three consecutive years, 1924-26. Only Arsenal (1933-35) and Manchester United (1999-2001 and 2007-09) have matched this since.

Right: War not only stifled social life and normal life for many people but also mothballed many traditions which were normal in peace time. Here we see the 7th Duke of Wellington's Regiment bringing out the colours, which had been stored during World War II. These proud gentlemen, marching in plain clothes in 1948, were probably veterans of the two great wars. Behind the regular army has always stood the volunteer movement, consisting of part time soldiers whose prime role was home defence. The background to this great regiment goes back a long way as during the Napoleonic Wars, in particular, the volunteer movement was very active. A Halifax Volunteer Corps was raised in 1794 "for the defence of the town, parish and neighbourhood of Halifax". In 1908 the volunteers, ceased to exist, but invited to transfer to the newly formed Territorial Force. The 2nd battalion became the 5th and 7th Battalions DWR based in Huddersfield. During the Great War a second and third battalion was raised and all served with distinction. In 1921 the Territorial Force became the Territorial Army with the 7th battalion fighting as infantry during World War II.

Below: What are they looking at? It was the aftermath of a very tragic day in Huddersfield's history. It followed a stake-out by police at a farm in Kirkheaton in July 1951. A disturbance in the early hours of the morning resulted in a police Inspector being shot dead and a constable receiving gun shot wounds to his lower body. This turned into a full scale operation with armed police finally arresting a man around 5.30am. Neighbours confirmed he had been led away in handcuffs. The constable was able to provide evidence at a special court held at his bedside but sadly later died. The detained man was charged with and found guilty of a double murder, at Leeds Assizes and subsequently executed. It is hard to believe that the onlookers, children included, could be witnessing the events of such a brutal and sad day in their local town.

Left: The Imperial Arcade in May 1953 looked even more splendid when dressed in flags and bunting for the coming coronation of Queen Elizabeth. The whole of the Commonwealth was represented in the display of flags and no doubt the tailor's shop owned by Mr Silver would have been doing a good trade in new suits for the celebrations, if money allowed.

Below: Hats and caps were still an important part of a man's attire, even on the bowling green, in August 1953. This shot was taken at Greenhead Park in what was probably the 'Holiday at Home' week for those who chose not to go away for their holiday. The park was first opened in 1884 for the public to enjoy. The original wooden pavilion for the bowlers was built in 1930s and demolished due to its deterioration in 2010.

1873
REBUILT
1930
LONG
HULA HULA
GIRL

Top left: To raise funds for charity the traditional 'Longwood Sing' was started in 1873 at Nab End Tower in Longwood. It was originally held on the second Sunday in August known as 'Thump Sunday' but later changed to the first Sunday in September. The Sing now forms the centre-piece of the Longwood Festival, with concerts in St Mark's Church and an art show in the Mechanics Hall.

Left: This fancy dress parade held at Primrose Hills Gala day in July 1953 shows the imagination of the children and their parents with Hula Hula Girls and the very smart Queen, Miss Joan Mathews. The coronation year was always one for celebration and these children have shown their support fully in that respect.

Above: A Christmas pantomime in Meltham, in December 1956 finds the Meltham Church Ladies performing a scene from Robin Hood with Maid Marion central to the plot. The all female cast will have maintained the tradition of pantomime by playing roles of both genders which may have been more of a challenge than normal given the characters of Little John, Friar Tuck and the Sheriff of Nottingham!

Right: The Town Hall offers facilities for a wide variety of meetings and functions in rooms that can be used from smaller gatherings to large public events, including conferences and weddings. It is very well suited to use as a concert hall. Huddersfield Choral Society, perhaps the best known of its type in the country, performs to sell-out houses here. Such is its reputation that Sir Malcolm Sargent, one of our foremost conductors, made a point of coming here in order to conduct the Society in moving performances of Handel's 'Messiah'. The Polish composer, Henryk Gorecki, was inspired to come in person to lead a performance of his Third Symphony. Since fully opening in 1881, many other famous names have taken the stage. Yehudi Menuhin, pictured, is one such superstar of music who has performed here. Born in New York in 1916, he was recognised as a talented violinist while just a child and was recording for HMV as a teenager in the 1930s. He became friendly with British composer Benjamin Britten in the 1940s and spent some time in this country. He established a music school in Surrey in 1962. Menuhin enjoyed a variety of music and was fond of mixing classical playing with jazz styles, something he did regularly with Stéphane Grapelli in the 1970s. Several British violinists, such as Nigel Kennedy and Nicola Benedetti, say that he was a strong influence in their musical development. Menuhin was still making recordings in 1999, the final year of his life.

Did you know?

Huddersfield Choral Society, recognised as the UK's leading Choral Society, was founded in 1836.

Left: The BBC came to Huddersfield in May 1968 to record the Huddersfield Choral Society at the Town Hall. Founded in 1836, Huddersfield Choral Society has an international reputation as the UK's leading choral society, Huddersfield Choral Society was an early pioneer of recording, starting in 1927 with Columbia Records. The main organ at the back of the photo was named 'Father Willis' and was used in many major recitals and lunch time events.

Above: Huddersfield Town Hall was a popular venue for secondary schools' prize-giving days. This photo shows the speech day for Central (Kayes) College in May 1953, with the Mayor and Mayoress of Huddersfield at the prize-giving table at the front.

Right: Brass bands have always been popular in the Huddersfield district and Skelmanthorpe Band is one of the oldest in the country, formed in 1843. In 1993, the band celebrated its 150th anniversary in style by becoming the Third Section National Champions under the direction of Stuart Fawcett. Further success followed, resulting in the achievement of Championship Section status in January 2000.

Above: Which prize could I win? A question on the lips of each of the children as they consider their options in 1957 at the Huddersfield Sports Ground. How about a Sooty Stencil Set or a toy weaving loom or even a gingerbread baking kit? All were very practical toys which provided skills and learning together with fun and enjoyment. How would they compare, if at all, to an 'Xbox 360' or 'VMotion Video Game' or even a 'Halo 3 Laser Target Set'?

Bottom left: A Fancy Dress event brings out the very best in home made costumes. The children would have been fully involved in making these outfits and each would be their own favourite character from cartoons or children's comics. We can see Yogi Bear, Miss Quality Street, a Little Strawberry and Charlie Chaplin. It was a serious competition with three judges, two ladies and a gent!

Below: In the year that Queen Elizabeth was crowned and Sir Edmund Hillary and Sherpa Tensing successfully climbed Everest the Meltham Co-op had their Gala Day in June 1953. A very smart Austin Atlantic Convertible was passed by the procession and the boys, particularly were impressed by such a 'flash' looking car on their local streets.

Below: Sack races were a topical feature of the summer gala days and the lads here were having to cover some ground to be crowned the winner. A good crowd had gathered and other boys appear to be asking the suited gent if they could be in the next race. No doubt a well deserved ice cream from the van at top left was their next request.

Right: The ladies here are at the Huddersfield Town Hall and hoping their glamorous looks and summer frocks will help them become the Miss ICI of 1962. It is possible that these frocks were made of the newly developed fabric, Crimplene, which ICI had just brought out although the cloth was heavy, wrinkle resistant but retained its shape well. The California-based fashion designer Edith Flagg was the first to import this fabric from Britain to the USA. During the first two years, ICI gave Flagg a large advertising budget to popularise the fabric across America. The grand organ of the Concert Hall provided a magnificent backdrop to this beauty parade, all enhanced by spring flowers at the front of the stage.

Below: The domestic electrical era moved another relentless step forward with the re-opening of the Huddersfield Co-op store in New Street in November 1963. The electric ceiling lights were on display, but the two bar 'coal effect' electric fires, Morphy Richards electric blankets for the bed and Electrolux sweeper had their day 50 years ago.

Above: Loyalty cards and Nectar points prove there is nothing new in the world of retail. This photo of the Meltham Co-op Gala in 1953 was evidence of the importance of the Co-op's 'Divi' system whereby families could quote their divi number and receive dividends on their purchases which may have generally gone towards their summer holiday or break. Meltham Mills Provident and Meltham Industrial Co-op merged in 1927 and later in 1949 the Co-op National Membership scheme allowed families to obtain their divi from any Co-op not just their local store. The Meltham Society closed in 1969 and, sadly, there would be no more of these 'celebration gala days'.

Right: It doesn't seem that long ago since the government began to introduce its healthy eating approach as this youngster in the fancy dress milk bottle shows by promoting the 'Drink a Pint of Milk A Day'. This was when school milk was given to children free of charge to build strong bones and teeth. The governments' health campaign had clearly not gone as far as the lad colleting rags for balloons shows depicting a typical rag and bone man smoking his pipe. The Gala was held at Hopkinson's, one of several Huddersfield firms to hold annual events similar to this.

Below: There have been many landlords and landladies of the Rovers Return Inn so central to the Coronation Street TV series, but possibly none more memorable than Jack and Annie Walker. Annie was in the series' first episode in 1960 until she retired from the role 23 years and 1,746 episodes later in 1983. They are both seen here at the opening of the Huddersfield Co-op in November 1963. They can be seen here eating a packet of Golden Wonder Crisps, Walkers of course!

GETTING AROUND

Below: Joseph Brown was born on 18 November 1864 at Tydd St Giles, the most northern of all the villages in Cambridgeshire. He came to Huddersfield in c1883 and made his home in the Bradford Road area. Joe married Louisa Wood in May 1886 at St John's Parish Church. They had three daughters, Eliza, Emma and Lily. The family lived for a while at Lower Hagg in Netherthong before moving to Outlane, though by the time of the 1901 census there is no mention of Louisa. Perhaps she died in childbirth, a sadly common occurrence in Victorian times. Joe worked as a groom in the 1890s and was then employed by the Huddersfield Steam Laundry on Syringa Street in Marsh, just off what is now the A640, Westbourne Road. Large laundries were popular in the days before washing machines, twin tubs and tumble driers. If a family could afford to use the laundry facilities, it saved a lot of hard work and drudgery. In the 1930s, George Formby even managed to sing a popular song, 'Chinese Laundry Blues', that based its theme on what many people called 'the steamie'. Actor James Mason was born in the Marsh area. He made the reverse journey to Joseph Brown when he went to Cambridge in the late 1920s to attend university.

Right: There is plenty for the rhubarb or rose grower to collect from the carriageway of Westgate. The droppings are ample evidence that good old Dobbin has not entirely had his day as a means of transport power. The policeman on point duty would have had a fairly simple job keeping things moving as there was not much else around to cause him problems. The tram had little choice when it came to the direction it was to go in. The tracks, cables and pantograph arm saw to that. Westgate runs across the town centre; today connecting one side of the ring road to the other. The scene must be from June 1911. The message 'God bless our king' on the left, on what is now Lloyds TSB at 1 Westgate, on the corner with Market Place, rather gives the game away. That and the flags fluttering in the breeze tell us the town was celebrating the coronation of King George V. He came to the throne in May the previous year on the death of his father, Edward VII. Rushworth's department store stood for many decades on the opposite corner at 1 John William Street. It is now Nando's, a restaurant specialising in Portuguese dishes. You won't see Father Christmas in there as you used to do when it was Rushworth's.

CHINA
Rushwo
LINDLEY
Bags & Trunks

Above: The inside of a station with such a grand facade did not quite live up to expectations, however the platforms at Huddersfield Station were there to serve a practical purpose. The steam locomotive standing at the platform could have been taking holiday makers to the coast, but more likely as the large clock on the opposite platform shows 4.10pm, local travellers may have been heading homeward.

Below With a complete lack of any evidence of motorised transport in view, we must be looking at a scene from the latter days of the Victorian age when the horse was still the main source of power for road vehicles. For transporting people and goods over longer distances, the noble steeds had long since handed over the reins of dominance to the steam driven locomotives on the railways. Huddersfield Station in St Georges

Square was designed by JP Pritchett and built by Joseph Kaye. It began operating services in August 1847. The handsome frontage even moved the former poet laureate, Sir John Betjeman, to say that it was 'the most splendid in England'. This was praise indeed from the man who had also invited bombs to rain down on Slough in one of his poems. Another fan of the building called it 'a stately home with trains in it'. One of the adjacent pubs keeps a connection with the old days in its name, the Head of Steam. Traditionalists yearn for the days when there was such a thing. The station was refurbished in 2009 and the area in front of the station was extensively pedestrianised a few years ago.

Did you know?

Sir John Betjeman, Poet Laureate, described Huddersfield Railway Station as 'the most splendid façade in England' second only to St Pancras, London

Top: The world they knew would greatly change in a few years' time. Pictured before the outbreak of the 1914-18 War, some of them would don a uniform when Kitchener pointed his finger at them from the recruiting poster that said that their country needed them. Whether or not they returned, the face of their homeland would have altered. The horse pulling the wagon would have been sent to the knackers' yard and been replaced by a shiny motor lorry. The men were employees at the mill owned by Kaye and Stewart. This was a place where it was weaving sheds, joinery shops, looms, spinning frames, finishing areas, dyeing rooms and all manner of processes demanded by the textile trade. Although there was some silk and cotton produced, Huddersfield's mills were largely given over to working with wool. The grassland on the hills and slopes around the town was especially suited to the grazing of sheep. There was an abundance of water in the vicinity, useful for driving early machinery as well as for the fulling and dyeing processes. The water also contained the sort of subtle acids helpful in wool washing. A large supply of coal from rich seams was on hand when the industrial revolution fully took hold. The history of weaving has kept quiz setters happy. After a couple of pints in the pub it is not easy to recall Crompton's mule, Hargreaves' jenny and Cartwright's power loom without getting one mixed up with the other. Now then, which one is weft and which one warp?

Right and below: The Huddersfield Narrow Canal runs for about 20 miles from the Aspley Basin to link with the Ashton Canal at Whitelands Basin on the other side of the Pennines. The journey by barge is a lengthy one as it involves passing through 74 locks. The Standedge Tunnel at Marsden that takes the canal through the hillside is one of the most famous feats of Georgian engineering. It took 17 years to complete and opened in 1811. At three miles in length it is not only the longest, but also the deepest and highest canal tunnel in the country. This stretch of waterway was photographed where it reached Slaithwaite, about two and a half miles from Standedge on the Huddersfield side. Pictured in c1910, men, boys and animals worked in harmony with their barges. When they reached the tunnel, the lack of a towpath meant that men had to "leg" the barge through while the horses were walked over the hills to the other end. The canal operated commercially until 1944, though it had struggled to be profitable for some time before then. It fell into disrepair, but was restored by the Huddersfield Canal Society's hard work and reopened in 2001 for use by pleasure craft. The Narrow Canal is now part of the South Pennine Ring that also takes in the Rochdale Canal and sections of the Ashton Canal, Huddersfield Broad Canal and the Calder and Hebble Navigation.

Below: Living on a narrow boat for some has become a permanent way of life. A number of people have made their homes on these craft at fixed moorings. In the golden age of the canals, from the late 18th to the early 20th century, whole families had a life afloat when mixing work with domesticity. First it was the railways that took trade away from the waterways, and then it was road transport when motor lorries began moving goods. Eventually, many canals just died. It was not until the 1950s that interest in restoring them for leisure use really took off. Thanks to the tremendous efforts of volunteers and interested bodies, rotting lock gates were repaired, canal beds dredged and towpaths brought back into use. The Huddersfield Broad Canal was one of those that never closed, though at just under four miles in length it was easier to maintain than some. Formerly the Sir John Ramsden Canal, it was completed in 1780 and connects the Calder and Hebble Navigation at Cooper Bridge with the Huddersfield Narrow Canal at Aspley Basin. The site was laid out with wharves, cranes and housing for canal workers, creating a small dockland. Mills and warehouses were built close by. Little remains of its links with the industrial revolution. Seen here in 1992, it is now a small marina that attracts many visitors on sunny days and has refreshments available close by for those casual callers.

Above: Presently, the Three Nuns pub and restaurant occupies a prime spot at Cooper Bridge close to Junction 25 of the M62 on Leeds Road, in between Bradley and Mirfield. The site has links with an inn here that dates back to the end of the 15th century. Back at the start of the 20th century it was a popular watering hole for locals who turned up on foot or by horse and cart. The pub got its name after nuns from the nearby Kirklees Priory took refuge under its roof in the 1530s. This was a period when King Henry VIII set about the dissolution of the monasteries. Some claim that the place is haunted and that they have seen a dark figure rocking in a corner. One wag countered that by saying that he had spotted Anton Du Beke waltzing in the other. What cannot be denied is that it was a fine place to take refreshments over a century ago and is just as welcoming today. It is often used by walkers taking a break from their stroll to find the place nearby where some think that Robin Hood was buried. The Three Nuns underwent major refurbishment in 2007.

Below: At the time this photograph was taken, modes of transport in Huddersfield town centre included the bicycle, growing in popularity since pneumatic tyres had been brought in, the ever-present horses and carts transporting all kinds of products and materials, and, of course, the public tram. We can just see a policeman in the centre of the picture with arms crossed behind his back, seemingly more interested in the photographer than ensuring the horse doesn't hit the tram. The pedestrians likewise have also noticed the photographer and the young man with the newspaper bag around his neck walks casually along with his hands in his pockets.

Did you know?

The oldest pub in the town centre is the Parish (formerly the Fleece Inn) which has been trading since 1720.

The supporters waited patiently in line for the trams that would take them to the Leeds Road stadium, the home of Huddersfield Town FC. The interwar years were among the best that the club has ever known. During this period, it won the FA Cup, the Division One title on three consecutive occasions, set a club record with a 10-1 win over Blackpool in 1930 and packed in over 67,000 spectators to watch a quarter final cup tie against Arsenal. Leeds Road had a large capacity and was often used as a neutral venue for cup semi finals. You got to the ground early in those days to make sure of a decent view from the terraces. If you were among the first to be travelling to the ground, there was just a chance that you might be on the same bus or tram as one of the players. Their fixed wages were not enough for them to splash out on fancy cars and the like. They were only a bit better paid than the ordinary working man. With the occasional exception, football matches kicked off at 3 pm. There was no lunchtime or teatime soccer and no Sunday or Monday night matches kicking off to suit satellite TV.

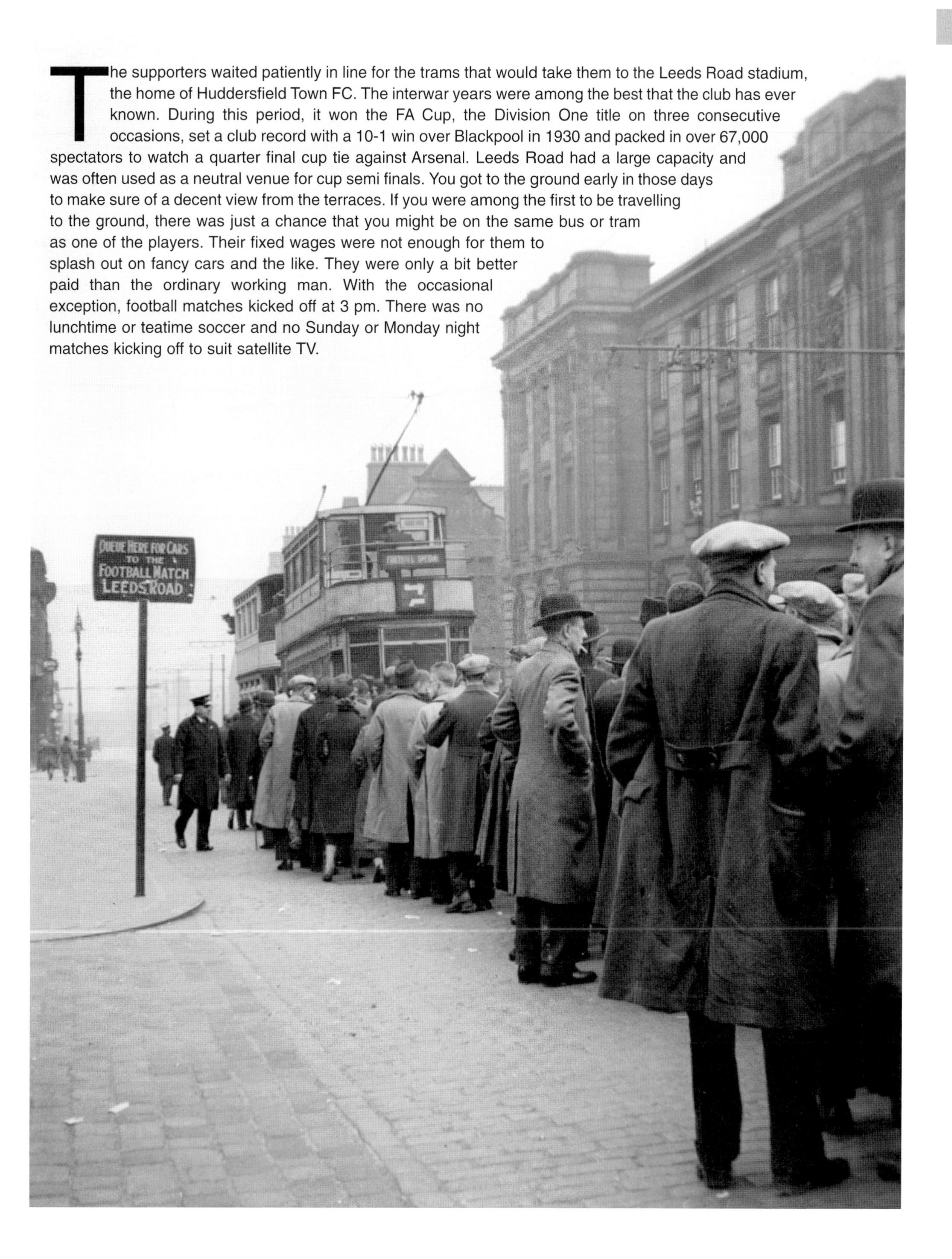

Above: It may well have been Good Friday on 21 April, 1905, but it did not turn out to be the best of days for those travelling on the Lancashire and Yorkshire Railway passenger train that was involved in this accident. A locomotive belonging to the London and North Western Railway had failed to observe a stop signal. The result was inevitable. The collision was head on and at speed. When looking at the devastating results of the crash, it is remarkable that only two passengers lost their lives. There were nine other casualties who needed hospital treatment. Both sets of drivers and firemen also received serious injuries. Travel by the railways is a comparatively safe way of getting around. However, a major crash is always big news. The first fatality of rail travel occurred somewhat perversely on the day that the Manchester to Liverpool route opened on 15 September, 1830. William Huskisson MP, a former Leader of the House of Commons, stumbled when trying to board a carriage and fell under the wheels of a locomotive. Other notable disasters before this one at Huddersfield included that at the Tay Bridge where 75 died in 1879 and near Armagh in 1889 when 79 perished. The biggest loss of life on an English railway in the 19th century took place on Christmas Eve 1874 when 34 died at Shipton on Cherwell, Oxfordshire.

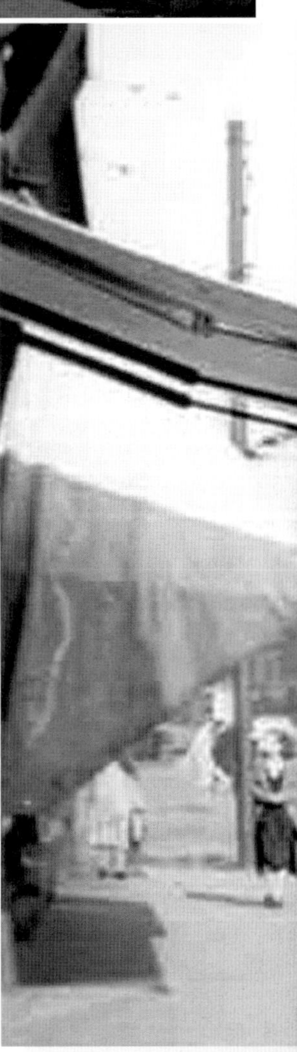

Did you know?

The three wheel 'LSD', commonly known as the rarest car in Britain, was built in Huddersfield just after the Great War and now can be seen in the Tolson Historical Museum.

Bottom left: This was the first trolley bus to run to West Vale and is seen arriving at Ainley Top, near where Junction 24 of the M62 can now be found, having made the climb up from the town centre. At least it was downhill all the way from here. This was not a particularly productive route and was one of the first to be axed in the early 1960s when this form of transport was gradually run down. Even so, it had served the locality for around a quarter of a century. The demise of the West Vale service was accelerated by its cost. Trolley buses consumed more power than trams and those needing to climb hills used up more than their fair share. Extra sub–stations had to be provided to make sure that sufficient power was available where it was needed. The life of trolley bus systems varied from town to town. Ours had a life of 35 years, but in neighbouring Halifax they had the briefest of life spans from 1921 to 1926. Yet, just a few miles away in Bradford a service operated for a staggering 61 years until 1972, making it Britain's longest running by far. To complete the pattern, just head a little further up the road to Leeds and there the trolley buses had all gone by 1928.

Below: Is the West Vale tram we can see here on time arriving in Westgate? We will never know, but it does seem pretty full with the chap just boarding at the back and standing passengers upstairs. Huddersfield's last tramcar ran to Brighouse in June 1940, with a subdued ceremony because of the wartime blackouts. Hardly a fitting tribute for a service which had served the community of Huddersfield so well for forty years.

Above, below and top right: The vehicle in St George's Square was one of those that were part of street life in the 1930s. In some areas trolley buses provided a bridge between the era of the tram and that of the motor bus as they overlapped both the earlier and later modes of public transport. In fact, for a while all three worked together in meeting passenger needs in and around our town. The Corporation had been granted powers to introduce motor buses within the borough in 1913, the outbreak of war the following year rather put things on hold. After the Armistice in late 1918, the new style of transport developed its routes and, by 1920, was allowed to ply its trade on a number of specified routes outside the borough boundaries. Trams continued in operation side by side with the buses, but track renewal was becoming expensive. When the line to Almondbury required replacement in 1933, the decision was made to use trolley buses instead. The route from Byram Street was inaugurated in December, using six new vehicles. The services to Lindley and Outlane were converted the following year. By April 1935, a decision to abandon the tramway was made. In 1937, the tramway conversion scheme was well under way as a large fleet of Karrier trolley buses was commissioned. However, they could not operate on the Honley route beyond Lockwood Church because of a low bridge on Woodhead Road, but by the time that World War II began only the Brighouse

service remained awaiting conversion. This was completed on 30 June 1940, the day after the final tram journey was made. Trolley buses operated from the depot at Longroyd Bridge and provided excellent service during the war, often carrying heavy passenger loads. They continued to serve Huddersfield well until the 1960s. The cost of replacing worn out overhead cabling and the increasing price of electricity rendered the vehicles uneconomic. From 1962 onwards, they were gradually phased out. The last one ran on the Waterloo to Lindley and Outlane route on 13 July, 1968. Several of our old friends can be found in the transport museum at Sandtoft, Lincolnshire.

Right: After World War II cars were becoming more popular and available and styles began to change. This popularity saw the growth of car showrooms around the Huddersfield area. Huddersfield had in fact a claim to car manufacturing through David Brown Gears 'Valveless cars' built in 1908 -1915 and the little know LDS car maker at Mirfield. The picture here shows the very modern looking showroom of Brockholes Motor Company on Westgate in Huddersfield, in stark contrast to the Victorian buildings further along. The Ford Popular which can be seen at the front of the showroom was Britain's lowest priced car when launched at around £390 including taxes and not a bad fuel consumption either at 36.4mpg.

Above: It took a group of Polish Troops to help clear the A62 at Standedge in February 1947. The main route between Huddersfield and Manchester at the time, the A62 was the arterial route relied upon by so many companies to move their goods westwards. Many of the lorries had been stranded for several days on a road only 10 miles from the centre of Huddersfield, but with the altitude and snow line at this point, it was always susceptible to the extremes of Yorkshire Pennine weather.

Bottom left: Holme Moss, another high point in the Huddersfield district, was a further route to suffer from the heavy snows of January 1952. This snow plough is trying hard to keep the road open to the television station. Not quite the Arctic, but the technicians at the television station had to keep supplies of food and blankets for these occasions. The BBC minibus which ferried them up to their place of work, would not have made it through these deep drifts of snow although Mr H Armitage, a driver of the minibus at the time, did his best to get through whenever possible.

Below: It was, of course, not only lorries which became stranded on the A62, but private cars as well, as can be seen in this shot from March 1953. There were no mobile phones at the time and if you did become stuck in the snow it was likely that you would have to trudge to the nearest phone box, with fingers crossed that the lines were not down, and try to get a message home. Another factor was that most cars did not have heaters at the time which would make it an even more inhospitable place to be.

Above: Heavy snows around Huddersfield seemed to be a constant weather pattern and certainly the driver of this Concrete Utilities vehicle from Hertfordshire would have felt so in 1953. Stuck in the drifts in freezing cold weather was not much fun and more than likely very costly for the driver who, depending on his employers, may have only been paid wages on delivery. Spare a thought for the photographer also, who was called out by the local newspaper to capture these scenes, with a heavy box camera and glass negatives.

Below: Again the road to Holme Moss becomes blocked in March 1953. What appears to be an Austin A40 finds itself stuck although the road has been previously cleared to a small extent. The cost of such a vehicle at the time would have been around £550 including taxes although the 948cc engine and 13 inch wheels would not have made much impression in such deep snow. The passenger looks a little forlorn and may be wondering where his driver has gone.

Above: George D James set up the Wrekin Roadways company in Telford, using the name of the pre-Cambrian hill in Shropshire as the inspiration for the name of his firm. For a while it was a major force on the road building and heavy haulage scene, before being bought out by Wynns in c1980. The huge vehicles seen at West Slaithwaite, overlooking the rolling countryside, included the 240 ton Contractor on the left. This was one of the Scammell range of heavy plant. This company was in business from 1921 until 1988. Other models of lorries and lowloaders that it manufactured were given sturdy sounding names, such as Commander, Constructor and Crusader.

Left and below left: This scene shows the ultimate demise of one of Huddersfield's newer trolley buses in February 1967. As with many accidents it is not just one aspect which is the cause, but a build-up of several. In this case on the Longwood route, the No 634 was following a turning procedure on the specially built platform (which had replaced the original hand-winched turntable) at Dodlee terminus, but unfortunately this one missed the platform whilst reversing and ended up in a field between an electricity sub-station and a stone wall. A 25-Ton crane was brought in to lift the damaged bus back onto the road but the overhead line had to be first removed in what was a fairly complicated recovery. Sadly, one of the newest models in the Corporation's fleet was deemed beyond repair and had to be scrapped.

Above: Hanson's began operations in the mid-1800s moving wool and textiles between Longwood and Huddersfield. They received many awards for their display of horses and horse vans at local shows and were always proud owners of heavy horses. This picture was taken in Cloth Hall Street in 1958 but these horses could be seen around the streets of Huddersfield well into the 1960s. Bill Hanson became an internationally famous horseman as a member of the British show jumping team and was a Master of Foxhounds. He sadly died in 1954 at the early age of 29.

Below: The horses took pride of place at the Hanson's Open Day in their new depot in Leeds Road in May 1962. Local deliveries by horse drawn vehicle were still made around the area although the larger motorised vehicles proved more efficient for heavy loads over longer distances.

AT WORK

Above: Clayton & Co (Huddersfield) Ltd played a leading part in Huddersfield during the First World War with their employees forming the Karrier division of St John Ambulance Brigade. They were set up to deal with any emergencies that

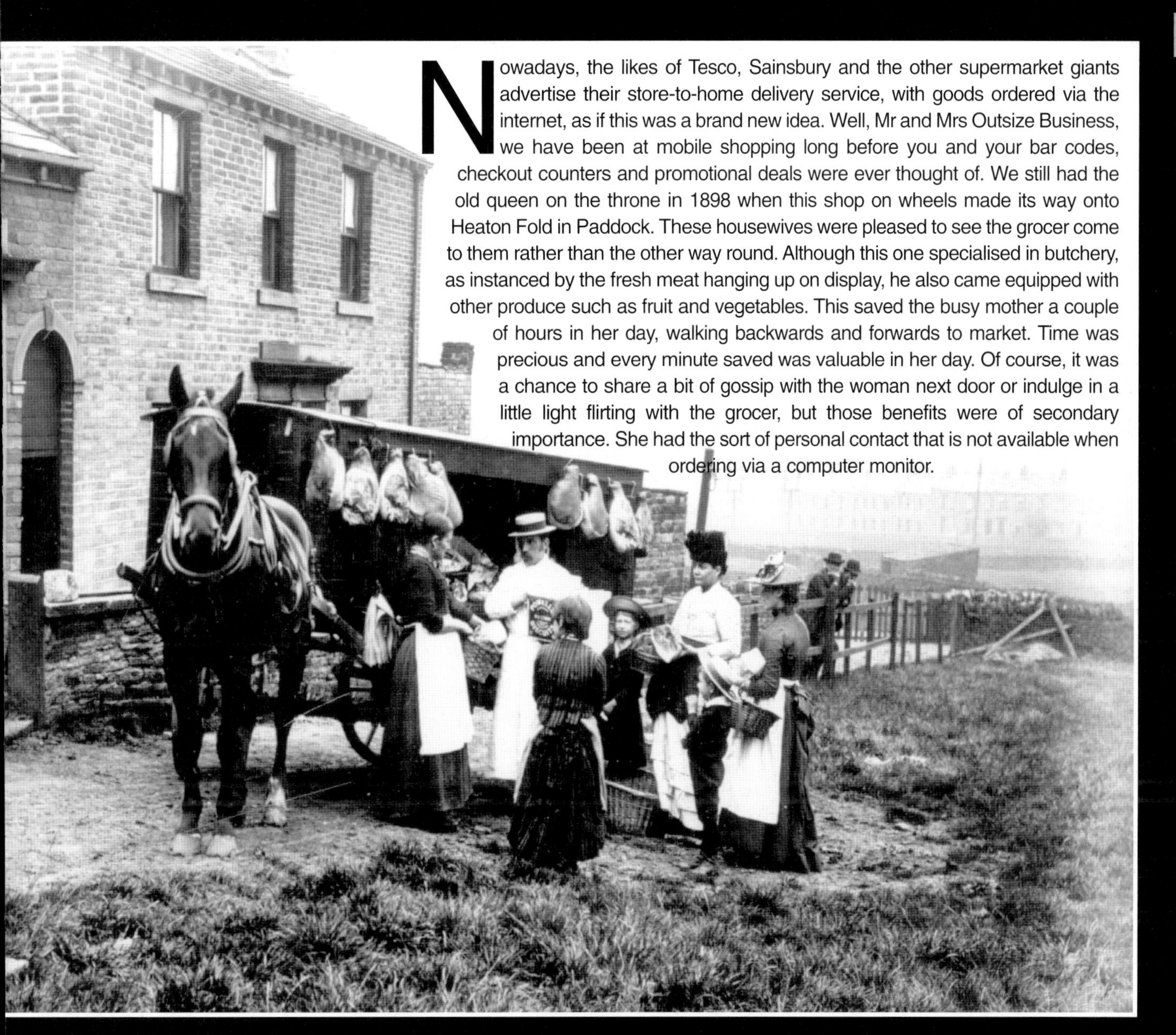

Nowadays, the likes of Tesco, Sainsbury and the other supermarket giants advertise their store-to-home delivery service, with goods ordered via the internet, as if this was a brand new idea. Well, Mr and Mrs Outsize Business, we have been at mobile shopping long before you and your bar codes, checkout counters and promotional deals were ever thought of. We still had the old queen on the throne in 1898 when this shop on wheels made its way onto Heaton Fold in Paddock. These housewives were pleased to see the grocer come to them rather than the other way round. Although this one specialised in butchery, as instanced by the fresh meat hanging up on display, he also came equipped with other produce such as fruit and vegetables. This saved the busy mother a couple of hours in her day, walking backwards and forwards to market. Time was precious and every minute saved was valuable in her day. Of course, it was a chance to share a bit of gossip with the woman next door or indulge in a little light flirting with the grocer, but those benefits were of secondary importance. She had the sort of personal contact that is not available when ordering via a computer monitor.

might arise due to the conflict. They were named after their place of work, Karrier Works, and were supplied with a vehicle and kit by the company. Their role was to transport the wounded from the railway station to the various Military Hospitals in the area, the main one being at Royd's Hall, Paddock and smaller ones such as the Holmfirth Military Cottage Hospital instigated by Doctor Williams which opened with six patients at a rent free house in Landsdowne Terrace, Holmfirth.

Left: Huddersfield Fire Station opened at Outcote Bank in 1961. The men in the service seen here would have hung up their helmets many a moon ago as this was 1899. The latest modern design of fire appliance was displayed for the general public to admire. From the time in the late 1820s that Braithwaite and Ericsson first coupled a steam engine to a fire pump, thousands of machines were built in Britain, primarily by two firms: Merryweather and Sons and Shand Mason and Company. The middle years of the Victorian era are famous for the way in which steam was used to power rail locomotives and great ocean going liners, but it was not all track and sea. The insurance companies' fire services, and those later taken over by local authorities, deployed steam engines that were horse drawn to the site of the blaze. It was from here that the engines kicked into action, producing enough power to send water jetting hundreds of feet into the air. The firefighters, or firemen as they were simply known back then, stood proudly, dressed in their full uniforms. The magnificent helmets, though, would prove to be a problem. With the more widespread use of electricity in homes and factories, the dangers from live cables making contact with the fancy metalwork on the headwear in a wet environment gave rise to a number of tragic accidents. Not surprisingly, a new style of safety helmet was soon introduced.

Below and inset: Nursing young children can be most rewarding, but also extremely distressing. The wellbeing of the next generation is always uppermost in our minds, but to members of the profession entrusted with the care of the sick, then physical needs are of paramount importance. When a child is nursed back to health or makes a dramatic recovery from some awful illness, then it is cause for rightful celebrations. Yet, there is that sad other side to the coin. The loss of a young life is terrible for all concerned. It takes a special sort of person to be able to cope with the ups and downs, the highs and lows of the children's ward. It was in the mid 1930s that Holmfirth toddler Margaret Ludlam, later Laherty, was a patient on the Children's Ward at the Royal Infirmary. She is the toddler in the nurse's arms. Fortunately, her problems were to do with an ear complaint, so she was soon on the mend. The hospital was the second of three to be referred to as the Huddersfield Royal Infirmary. The one that cared for Margaret first saw the light of day in 1831 and continued to serve the town until 1966, being replaced by the new building on Acre Street, Lindley, that began accepting patients the previous year.

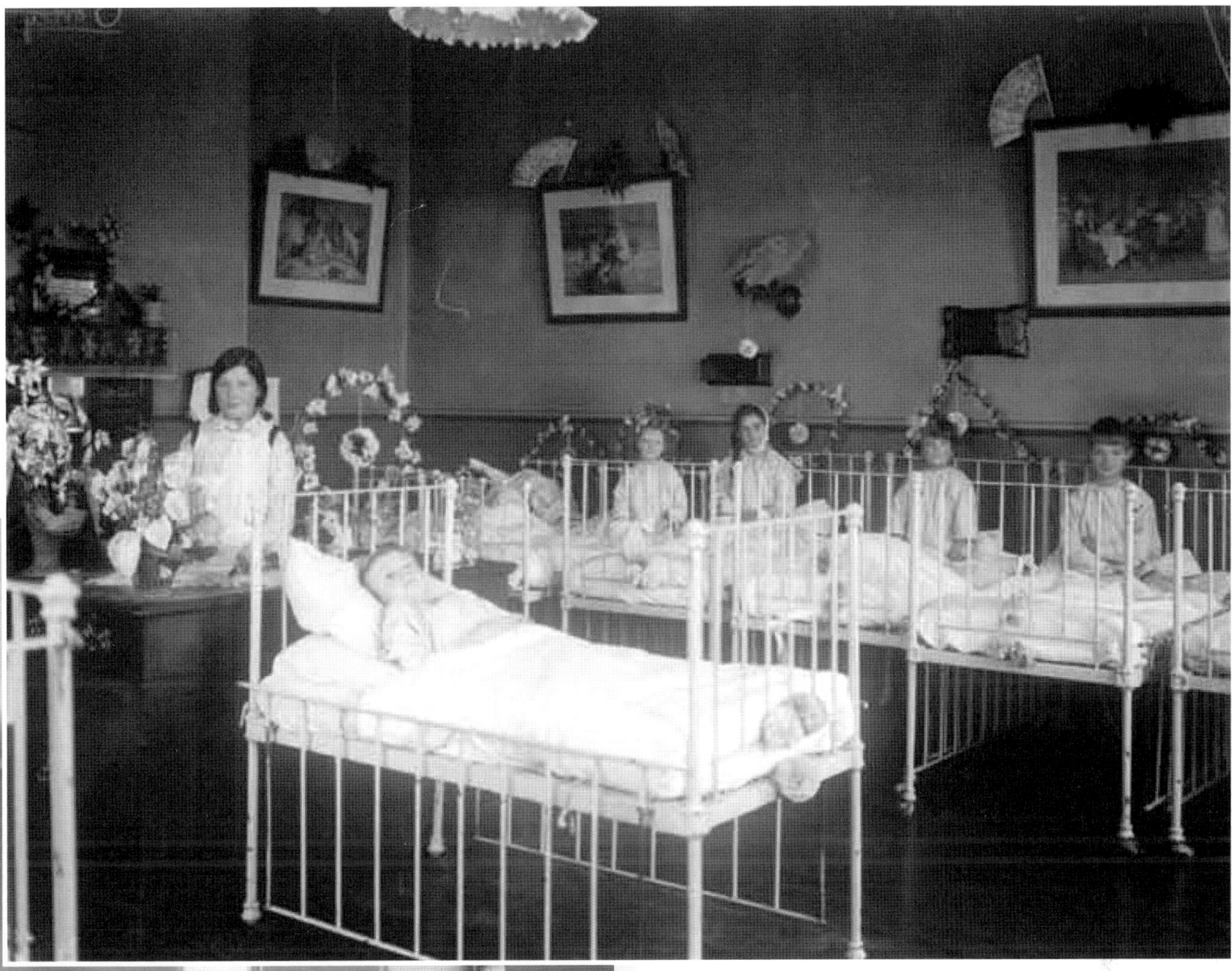

Above: The kiddies on the Royal Infirmary Children's Ward looked, in the main, to be getting on reasonably well, though one or two seemed to be struggling slightly. At least the bright flowers, decorations and pictures might have helped cheer them up a bit. Youngsters find it difficult to understand things like bed rest, whereas as we get older we are looking for more and more of it, though not necessarily in hospital. The ward gives the appearance of being full to bursting, with the beds crammed tightly together. There was not much chance of a bit of privacy, that is for sure. Still, at least there was the opportunity to have a chat with the occupant of the neighbouring bed. There were few others with whom to converse. In 1920, visiting hours were brief and the times strictly enforced. There was very little chance of a mum being able to stay over with a poorly child. Additionally, if Great Auntie Ivy was up from the Midlands, then she could not pop in and pay a call to the bedside on her arrival in town. She had to wait until the allotted hour. Otherwise, the dour presence of Sister and the giving of 'the look' that said it all would soon be employed. Even worse, it might be Matron and then banishment for life was on the cards! The image of Hattie Jacques in the 1972 film 'Carry On Matron' springs to mind.

Above: This trio were time served joiners, used to working in wood with hand tools and the most rudimentary of machinery to help them with their craft. This was 1910 when the brief Edwardian age came to an end with the death of Edward VII who passed away after a nine year reign. He provided the link between the old ways and the new that would come to pass in the lifetime of George V. Many changes lay ahead, including the outbreak of the Great War. That was only four years away and, with the death and destruction it brought, would provide the impetus for many new technologies in manufacturing. In the joinery shop at Kaye and Stewart's Rashcliffe Mill, Lockwood the talk about current events hinted at things to come. Instead of worrying about the quality and volume of the broadwoven cloth that the textile company produced, these chaps nattered away about the German Zeppelin that had made its maiden commercial flight. They spoke in awe about the wireless telegraphy that had helped ensnare the murderous Dr Crippen and marvelled that Henry Ford had sold 10,000 motor cars that year. Before long the skies, the roads and the airwaves would be full with varying types of traffic. Queen Victoria and her age was a long time past.

Did you know?

Huddersfield was at the centre of civil unrest in the Industrial Revolution with Luddites destroying mills and attacking Rawfords Mill owner, William Cartwright.

Top right: There were once dozens of textile mills in and around the town. You would be hard pressed to find more than two or three still in operation today, even those that tend to aim for a specialised market. Yet, this part of West Yorkshire, along with neighbouring Bradford and Halifax, was among the world leaders in this trade a few generations ago. Our town is handily placed at the confluence of the Colne and Holme rivers. Valley dwellers in days of yore came to realise that the waters that

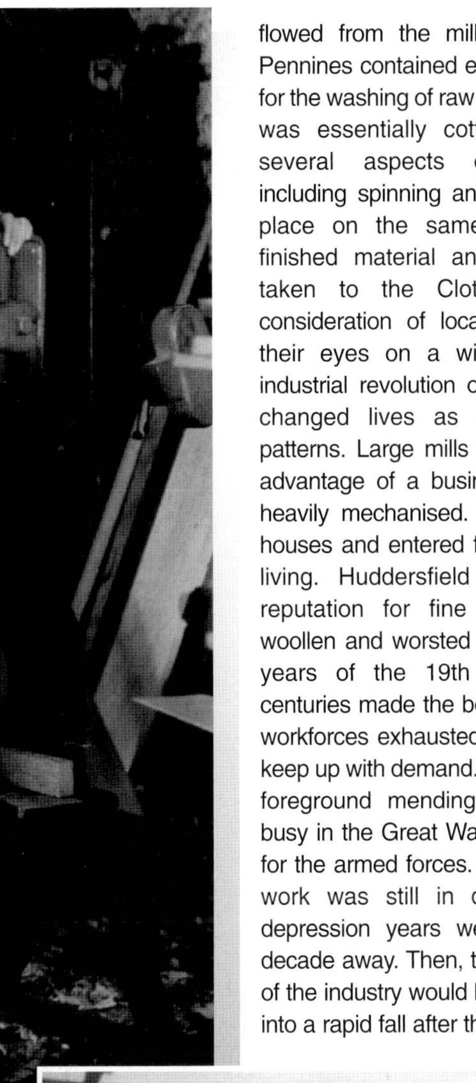

flowed from the millstone grit of the Pennines contained excellent properties for the washing of raw wool. The industry was essentially cottage based with several aspects of manufacture, including spinning and weaving, taking place on the same premises. The finished material and products were taken to the Cloth Hall for the consideration of local merchants with their eyes on a wider market. The industrial revolution of the early 1800s changed lives as well as working patterns. Large mills were built to take advantage of a business that became heavily mechanised. Workers left their houses and entered factories to earn a living. Huddersfield soon gained a reputation for fine workmanship in woollen and worsted goods. The boom years of the 19th and early 20th centuries made the bosses rich and the workforces exhausted as they strove to keep up with demand. The woman in the foreground mending cloth had been busy in the Great War making uniforms for the armed forces. Now, in 1920, her work was still in demand, but the depression years were only about a decade away. Then, the gradual decline of the industry would begin and carry on into a rapid fall after the next war.

Below: Quarmby and Sykes of Huddersfield were established in 1868, moving to their Dye house in Linthwaite in 1873. After a solid start they moved to Spinksmire Mill, in Meltham, where this picture was taken in 1936. It shows the 'pulling' department, a process used in processing wool and textile waste. In their catalogue of the same year they describe themselves as 'Manufacturers of Wool Waste. Extracts, Mungoes,Merinoes, Stockings, Carbonizers and Dyers', a fairly complete description you have to admit.

Below: The picture shows the hard work taking place at Benjamin Crooks Leather Tannery in the early part of the twentieth century. The sewing machines were an integral part of the making of footballs and other leather goods for a company later to become known as Mitre Sports International Ltd. Mitre started using its knowledge in leather for football and rugby in the 1880s and through expansion and acquisitions, widened its sporting portfolio to golf, squash, cricket, badminton and tennis.

Did you know?

Huddersfield University is the largest employer in the town and has over 23,000 students.

Right: A further, albeit earlier, photo of workers stitching leather footballs together at Benjamin Crooks Ltd.

Bottom right: It's not easy at first to identify the object in the picture, a torpedo or an underwater bomb, perhaps? It is in fact an 'X Craft' midget submarine designed to be towed to its intended area of operations by a full-size 'mother' submarine. It would have had a 'passage crew' on board whilst being towed at which point the operational crew would transfer. This crew

had to be hand selected as they could expect to be in the 51ft long vessel for up to 14 days at a time. Thomas Broadbent and Sons Ltd, a major Huddersfield engineering company, built four of these submarines around 1943 and it goes without saying that it had to be in total secrecy. Two of them were used in Operation Gambit, the landings in Northern France, and marked the extreme left and right flanks of the British and Canadian invasion beaches.

Syngenta in Huddersfield

Helping Farmers Feed the World

The world's population increases by approximately 8,500 people each hour of each day. Every second - in the time it takes for you to click your fingers - there are another two extra people to feed and clothe.

The 6.5 billion people or so now inhabiting our planet rely on plants for food, clothing, fuel, shelter and medicine and it is vital to ensure that the world's crops reach their true potential to meet the needs of this expanding world population.

Even today with modern farming methods, nearly one third of the world's crop production is still lost each year as a result of pests and diseases as less and less land has to provide for more and more people. Syngenta products give farmers greater crop yields which in turn, lead to greater availability of quality food and consequently lower costs for consumers.

The development of modern methods of crop protection has played an important role during the last century in ensuring the continued improvement required to feed a growing world population and to meet a greater demand by consumers for food higher in quality and in quantity.

The availability of a plentiful supply of fruit and vegetables, made possible by crop protection solutions and seeds varieties, has made a huge impact on human health in many countries over

the past few decades. Modern insecticides and other products are also helping to protect many millions of people across the world from health-threatening pests such as mosquitoes, cockroaches and rodents.

Left: *Syngenta's site pictured in 1905 whilst occupied by the Yorkshire Show's tents and marquees* ***Top and above:*** *Views of the plant in the 1940s.*

Sustainable Agriculture provides a balanced approach to meet present and future needs and seeks to tailor the best available technologies to provide solutions to farming problems. This is where Syngenta's commitment lies, continuously improving farming through Sustainable Agriculture. As part of sustainable systems, crop protection products - fungicides, herbicides and insecticides - are an essential part of modern agriculture. They contribute to dramatic increases in yields and bring other benefits to people and the environment, by helping to produce the food and cloth that is needed to sustain a world population of over six billion.

Today, in the 21st century, Syngenta is the flag-bearer for Huddersfield's internationally renowned chemicals industry. Over the course of the last one hundred years, thousands upon thousands of local people have worked at Syngenta's Leeds Road site. The skills and talents of these people have contributed for many years to world agriculture, playing an important role in bringing plant potential to life.

The history of the Syngenta Huddersfield site dates back to the First World War. And, under the ownership of pioneering and leading companies such as ICI, AstraZeneca and currently Syngenta, the Huddersfield site has long remained a key manufacturing centre for a wide range of chemical products, manufacturing for a global market.

Located in the foothills of the Pennines, Huddersfield is one of the largest towns in England and boasts a history of manufacturing excellence. During Victorian times Huddersfield was one of the most prolific producers of worsted cloth in the world. It was that excellence which prompted Read Holliday, a Bradford-born entrepreneur, to develop a range of dyestuff products to support the textile industry.

Manufacturing began when, at the age of 21, entrepreneur Read Holliday set up in business to distil ammonia at premises in nearby Tanfield. Holliday gave his name to the company which originally produced Naphtha in Huddersfield using the waste tar by-product from the local gasworks. To capitalise on the geography of his enterprise, he moved premises to sit alongside Huddersfield Gas Light Company on the east of the town centre at Turnbridge, off Leeds Road.

Although not a chemist himself, his ingenuity combined with his relationship with eminent chemists of the day enabled him to extend his range of coal tar by-products to the manufacture of early synthetic dyestuffs as well as ammonia, creosote, benzene and paint solvents.

Though by the end of the 19th century, Britain had a thriving

Top: *Entrepreneur Read Holliday.* ***Left:*** *Barrel coopers at work.* ***Above:*** *Washing down after a day in the Dyestuffs Division.*

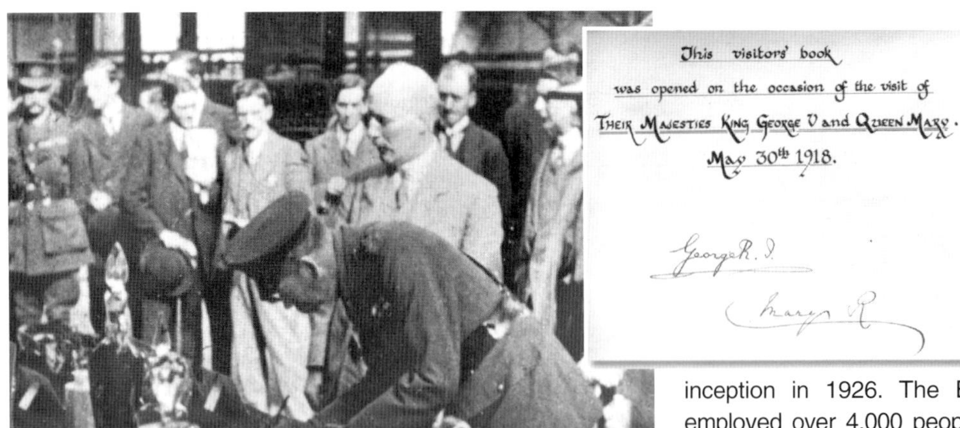

This visitors' book
was opened on the occasion of the visit of
Their Majesties King George V and Queen Mary.
May 30th 1918.

George R. I.
Mary R.

chemicals industry, the world leader at that time was Germany. German chemists had been at the forefront of many important scientific discoveries and industrialists had been quick to commercially exploit those developments to manufacture pharmaceuticals, synthetics and dyestuffs. Exports were vast and many other countries were heavily dependant upon imports of chemicals from Germany.

As a consequence of the outbreak of the First World War in 1914 there was an immediate shortage of key chemicals in Britain, not least those used to make dyes for military uniforms. The Government's strategy required a huge boost in British chemical production, covering all aspects of the industry and, in 1915, the Government of the day brought together leading chemical manufacturers, of which Holliday dyes was one, to create a national dye industry, British Dyes Ltd.

One of the sites acquired by British Dyes Ltd. was the 250 acre site at Leeds Road, adjacent to Holliday's Turnbridge Works and the manufacture of dyes began on what is now Syngenta's Huddersfield site.

On completing the construction and first manufacture at the Dalton Site in 1916, British Dyes Ltd. of Huddersfield, merged with Levenstein Ltd. in Blackley (Manchester) to form the British Dyestuffs Corporation, one of the four founder companies of ICI (Imperial Chemical Industries) at its inception in 1926. The British Dyestuffs Corporation Ltd employed over 4,000 people in Huddersfield, many of whom saw King George V and Queen Mary come to visit and see where the cloth dyes for British Army uniforms were being made.

Under the stewardship of ICI, production at Huddersfield diversified from dyestuffs to other chemical products. It became the first site to synthesise ethylene glycol used in anti-freeze and plastics. The site also became the first to manufacture Nylon outside of the USA; it also produced the world's first Terylene polymer for use in strengthening fabric. And inevitably, during the Second World War, its workers made a huge contribution to Britain's war effort.

In the 1960s and 1970s the Dalton Works continued to diversify, producing the world's first continuous manufacture of the biocide, Proxel. Huddersfield also made the world's first fibre reactive dyes, Procion, Disperse and Nylomine, which revolutionised cloth printing and fabric design.

Huddersfield's contribution to the British chemical industry had few boundaries - the site produced rubber stabilisers for the tyre industry as well as resins for the paint and finishes sector. Polyurethane

Top left: *King George signs the visitors' book on 30th May 1918.* ***Top left, inset:*** *The signatures of King George and Queen Mary.* ***Left:*** *Drums from 1940 labelled with their destination - places as far and wide as Buenos Aires to Bombay.* ***Above:*** *A filter press for filtration of final dyestuff.*

from rationalisation of the agrochemical business with the relocation of key products to Huddersfield from other ICI sites. A new product, Glyphosate would be a huge challenge for the site using complicated and innovative chemistry and whilst the manufacturing challenges were ultimately met, the commercial demand for Glyphosate changed and manufacture later ceased at Huddersfield.

The growth prospects of other products, such as Karate also brought expansion to the Huddersfield site – a successful product used (amongst other uses) to help the fight against diseases such as malaria carried by mosquitoes.

foam was manufactured for use in furniture, cars and electrical appliances. And the 1970s were capped by achieving the Queens Award for Technological Innovation for Reglone - a non-volatile herbicide for use as a pre-harvest aid to drying out certain crops in order to make harvesting easier.

In response to changing social needs and attitudes towards the chemical industry, the 1980s ushered in a new era of environmental awareness. Millions of pounds were invested in state-of-the-art waste management facilities.

And, as part of helping people understand the contribution made by the chemical industry, Huddersfield led the way by embarking on a series of public-facing initiatives, such as Open Days and Environmental Education Workshops for school children. Such activities helped local communities learn more about how the industry had changed and in particular, the high standards of operation.

In 1993, ICI began to 'demerge' and the site became a key manufacturing facility for Zeneca and later, AstraZeneca. Huddersfield benefited

When Syngenta was born in 2000, the award winning Huddersfield site focused the energy and talents of its staff on five key crop protection brands: Reglone, Gramoxone, Karate, Force and Fusilade.

Top left: *July 1951, workers making their way home on various modes of transportation.* ***Above left:*** *The Mayor of Huddersfield laying the foundation stone for the new office block in 1951.* ***Above:*** *An early view inside the administration block.* ***Below:*** *An aerial view of the works in the1960s.*

Since 2000 the long success story at Huddersfield has continued unabated. In 2005 the site won the Chemical Industries Association (CIA) Award for its manufacturing excellence. In 2006, staff won a global Syngenta Award. In 2007 they won the CIA Award for Effective Engineering and in 2008 the CIA Award for Responsible Care. In 2010 the site won a second CIA award for Excellence in Engineering.

Today, however, gone are the manufacture of dyes, colours and chemicals for textiles; in their place is one of the most technologically advanced production facilities in the UK, focused primarily on the manufacture of intermediaries for many leading crop protection brands.

Now part of the Syngenta family, employees at Huddersfield continue to be part of a long and illustrious story, sharing a common legacy of professional manufacturing – all on the Dalton site where it began so long ago with the aptly named colour patent 'Spirit Blue'. The spirit of today's employees and the blue and green of the Syngenta motif are a daily reminder of the past, and a promise to help growers around the world meet the challenge of the future - to grow more from less.

With a global marketing reach, Syngenta has become a major player in the fields of non-selective herbicides and insect control, and the business is investing in plant biotechnology to offer farmers alternative ways to protect and improve the yield and quality of their crops. As a leader in crop protection and as one of the top producers of high-value commercial seeds, Syngenta plays a key role in feeding and protecting the world.

Syngenta's success on a global platform is acknowledged locally too. As well as worldwide initiatives such as the Syngenta Foundation for Sustainable Agriculture, in the local community Syngenta

Top: *Syngenta's entrance, Leeds Road, Deighton.* **Above:** *Open day, 1986.* **Left:** *An Insecticides production plant.* **Bottom left:** *A herbicides production plant.* **Below:** *A view inside a production facility.*

helps deliver science and educational projects. Music and the arts are also part of Huddersfield's heritage and Syngenta has a history of supporting several local activities such as The Huddersfield Choral Society and The Lawrence Batley Theatre.

Syngenta continues its pursuit of innovative research and the application of modern technology to provide sustainable agricultural solutions. These solutions, along with Huddersfield's manufacturing excellence, allow growers across the world to realise the true potential of crops and to deliver high quality food for an ever-growing and ever more demanding world population.

Top left: *Planting a tree to celebrate the birth of Syngenta in 2000.* ***Left:*** *Syngenta employees from Huddersfield on a field trial visit.* ***Above:*** *Site Manager, Alistair Conn, (second left) pictured with Syngenta's new apprentices.* ***Below and bottom:*** *Awards won by Syngenta at the Chemical Industry Awards.*

Armitage Sykes LLP
Leading the Way

For over 250 years Armitage Sykes LLP has played a significant role in the communal and business life of Huddersfield. Now in the 21st century, the firm is one of the largest in the area, providing decisive legal advice, guidance and solutions to individual, business and organisational clients, all of whom who value the high standard of legal support the firm can provide.

The modern solicitor is the successor to three former ancient professions known as attorneys, solicitors and proctors. In earlier times these 'lawyers' assisted judges on the Kings Bench in the early stages of litigation, or carried out the less-skilled work in the ecclesiastical and Admiralty courts.

Successive reorganisations of the courts of law and of the legal profession have left us with just two kinds of lawyers: barristers and solicitors.

For most people barristers remain remote ethereal people whose work is seldom understood by those outside the law. By contrast solicitors are familiar folk with offices on every high street.

Sooner or later we all become involved in matters legal: making a will, buying a house or getting divorced. Few of us understand all the complexities involved in such issues, and expert advice is essential.

For those in business solicitors offer even more help: partnership agreements, company formation, debt collection, employment disputes and, sometimes, bankruptcy. Much effort and cost can be saved by seeking timely legal assistance at an early stage in such matters.

Top: *The firm's 72 New North Road premises.*

In Huddersfield one of the most familiar names is the firm of Armitage Sykes LLP, a firm of solicitors whose history in the town goes back far beyond the memory of anyone now living.

Indeed, almost as if to underline the point, the very names Armitage and Sykes are historically speaking two of the most common family names in the Huddersfield area.

As long ago as 1750 the forerunner of Armitage Sykes LLP solicitors were practising law in Huddersfield; back then however the name of the firm was Crosland & Fenton.

Today Crosland & Fenton's papers are held by the West Yorkshire Kirklees archive service. These records form part of the fascinating history of our town and its surrounding area. The papers include draft wills dating back to 1808; there are also court briefs for clients, including businesses and townships, dating from 1763 to 1840; there are deeds, rental and other papers relating to the Storthes Hall Estate from 1846 to1926; Penistone manor court baron rolls from 1811 to 1935; various clients' deeds, draft deeds and abstracts of title from as far back in time as 1718 - and including properties as far apart as Brighouse, Greetland, Heckmondwike, Mirfield, Rastrick, Saddleworth, Shelley, Shepley, Thurstonland, and, of course, every part of Huddersfield.

Not for them the modern day rush of completing complicated commercial transactions or handling tricky matrimonial disputes. More likely there would have been a leisurely and scholarly approach to the complex and arcane application of the law at that time. Justice and law have sadly not always been synonymous, still more so in those far off days. Mr Crosland practised from Deadmanstone near Berry Brow, Huddersfield, later moving to King Street. From that legal practice arose in due course the firm of Hall, Norton & Atkins who practised from 9, Station Street, Huddersfield until their amalgamation in 1993 with the younger, but still venerable, firm of Armitage, Sykes & Hinchcliffe.

Armitage, Sykes & Hinchcliffe, according to conversations recorded with Mr Paul Bradley and Mr Herbert E Walker, respectively Clerk and Articled Clerk (trainee solicitor) to Mr Walter Armitage, began life around 1850.

In the mid-19th century Mr Armitage lived as a country gentleman at Kirkstyles Farm, Cumberworth, a farm of about 70 acres in the southern rural outskirts of the town. He kept a fine table and a good cellar, but any money made in the law was lost on the farm. He made the journey from Cumberworth to Huddersfield astride a white horse which he stabled at a hostelry in Lord Street. It is said that Mr Armitage would fight a case all day for a guinea. Mr James Sykes joined him in 1891 and Mr AET Hinchcliffe soon after then.

Left and above: *Former members of Hall, Norton & Atkins.*

Until around this time the formal education of solicitors often left much to be desired.

In 1899, however, after earlier unsuccessful initiatives in 1879-80 and in 1888-89, law teaching was eventually introduced into the curriculum of the Yorkshire College (Leeds University's predecessor).

The Yorkshire Board of Legal Studies (representing local Law Societies) offered the College an annual grant of £450 if it would undertake to establish a Law Department in order to prepare candidates for University degrees and professional examinations.

Some 22 students were enrolled. Initially, most of the students were part-time non-degree students, who studied for one year in preparation for the Law Society's Intermediate Examination while working as articled clerks in solicitors' offices. There were only a handful of law degree students. They too also worked as articled clerks, while studying for three years for the degree which gave exemption from the Law Society's Intermediate Examination.

The Department's first graduate was James Sykes of Huddersfield, who passed the Final LL.B. examinations in June 1902.

James Armitage had died in 1898 (the day after he made his will - not a good example to his clients) and the office moved to 13, Westgate, subsequently a building society office, before moving to 1, Westgate over Lloyds Bank, where the firm would stay for some 60 years until 1973. It is said that there was considerable rivalry for the tenancy of 1, Westgate, which was then owned by the West Yorkshire Bank before its takeover by Lloyds. However, the fact that Mr James Sykes' uncle Sir Charles Sykes, of Brockholes, was a director of the bank may have made a difference.

Before the Great War of 1914-18 the personnel was all male - including the secretaries or clerks. But the outbreak of war in 1914 changed all that, and the first female secretaries started work in around 1920. The firm is perhaps more distinguished for providing one of the

Below *Armitage Sykes & Hinchcliffe circa 1910.*

first (of four) women to qualify as solicitors in 1925 - namely Mary Sykes. Women were in fact only permitted to become solicitors in 1922. Mary Sykes was the daughter of James Sykes and later went on to found her own practice. The story goes that she was eventually constrained to resign from the firm when AET Hinchcliffe persisted in correcting the duplicates of the letters she had sent the previous day - that was the final straw. In those days the senior partner still saw all the duplicates of letters sent from the office, no matter who had written them.

One of the consequences of the firm's great longevity is the inheritance of the management of ancient charitable trusts like the Godfrey Beaumont Charity, originally set up to provide a stipend for the parishes of Meltham and Honley. There was also the Robert Nettleton Charity founded in 1613. All that experience has been of considerable assistance in welding the present generation of lawyers into a cohesive team, with competence over a wide area of practice rarely found in a provincial town. The firm was even involved in 1853 in efforts to unseat the sitting Member of Parliament. History fails to relate the outcome of this, but it must have progressed quite far as there is a letter reporting the arrangements made for the various witnesses to travel to London for a hearing.

Lawyers most readily learn their trade by sitting at the feet of others in the firm who can show them how things are done. Old established firms can do this. But we must not look solely at the past. Modern technology, particularly the fulsome use of electronic messaging and the rapid exchange of information have transformed the way modern solicitors do business. Armitage Sykes LLP was the first legal firm in Huddersfield to embrace the computer, something which makes possible a far greater efficiency in dealing with the modern client's requirements in business and private matters.

Modern technology can help clients in many ways. Making a Will is a sensible thing to do as it ensures that your assets are shared in the way that people want them to be. But often the problem that relatives face is that they often know a Will was made but don't know which solicitor holds it or how to go about finding it.

Using an online database is a quick and easy way to find a Will and which solicitor is holding it. In 2010 Armitage Sykes Solicitors signed an online deal to help relatives quickly and easily find the Will and solicitor holding it.

Armitage Sykes, however, is not just about the law. The firm takes its involvement with the community seriously too, continuing to support many local hospices and charities including both Kirkwood and Overgate.

The firm supported the Yorkshire Air Ambulance's move to its new headquarters undertaking the legal work for the new building. Basharat Ali, partner, presented a cheque for £750 to Peter Sunderland, Chairman of Yorkshire Air Ambulance, at the official opening of the new Yorkshire Air Ambulance's HQ on 7th May, 2010.

Top left: *Walter Armitage, former partner of Armitage Sykes & Hinchcliffe.* ***Left:*** *Mr A.E.T Hinchcliffe.*

Basharat commented "We were delighted to be able to help Yorkshire Air Ambulance get its new headquarters up and running. It's been an exciting project to be involved with. The helicopters are on duty seven days a week, 365 days a year and this new facility will help provide cover to the region."

Armitage Sykes have supported Yorkshire Air Ambulance for a number of years and continue to raise funds through the "Bag it Up" scheme by recycling used printer cartridges.

Meanwhile reputation, service and standard of legal work count for a great deal.

In 2011 Armitage Sykes Solicitors became one of the first law firms in the country to secure Conveyancing Quality Scheme (CQS) status, the Law Society's new home buying quality mark.

Law Society president Linda Lee said the CQS award was recognition for the firm's high standards in residential conveyancing: "These first practices are the flag bearers of the CQS and this recognition of the quality of their service begins a new chapter in the home buying process. In what is already a crowded conveyancing market, CQS accredited legal practices will be clearly visible to any one looking to buy a home. For what is the most expensive purchase of anyone's lifetime, it is vital that they can rely on the quality service provision of CQS."

The previous year the firm had been awarded the Lexcel Standard by the Law Society. The Law Society explains "the Lexcel practice management standard is only awarded to solicitors who meet the highest management and customer care standards."

The firm has been meeting the legal requirements of the business community in and around Huddersfield for over 250 years. The current partners value the firm's hard-earned reputation and believe clients equally value the

Above: *Basharat Ali presented a cheque for £750 to Peter Sunderland, Chairman of Yorkshire Air Ambulance at the official opening of the new Yorkshire Air Ambulance's HQ on May 7, 2010.* ***Below:*** *Carol Dolman and Martin Thompson, Partner at Armitage Sykes received the Lexcel Standard from the Law Society in September 2010.*

service they provide. Many clients have worked with the firm through generations as it has progressed and kept ahead of the game in terms of technology, efficiencies and innovative ways of providing the services clients want in the timely and personal way they like to receive them. Armitage Sykes takes pride in providing decisive legal advice, guidance and solutions to individual business and organisational clients who value their high standard of legal support. Indeed, the firm has an enviable reputation for having its staff promoted into the judiciary.

Robert Turner, Senior Partner at Armitage Sykes, commented: "As a firm we concentrated on bringing in the right quality of people with good experience who understand what clients need and the matters they face in business.

The Ministry of Justice published research showing that over 80% of people didn't know if they had a good solicitor or not and often they find out when it's too late. Choosing the right solicitor is an important decision for any business."

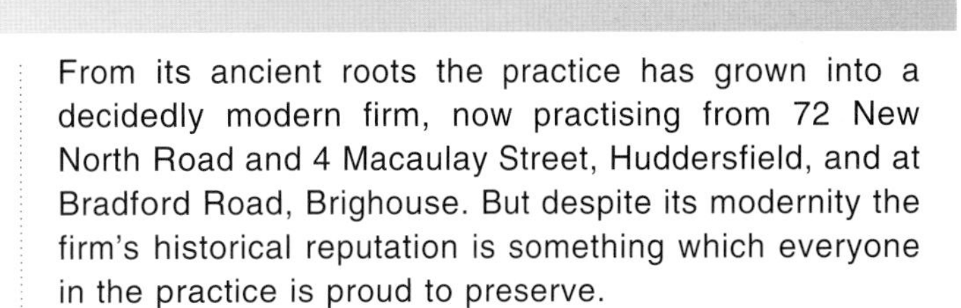

From its ancient roots the practice has grown into a decidedly modern firm, now practising from 72 New North Road and 4 Macaulay Street, Huddersfield, and at Bradford Road, Brighouse. But despite its modernity the firm's historical reputation is something which everyone in the practice is proud to preserve.

Today, Armitage Sykes LLP has expertise in over 44 specialist legal areas through its seven departments. The experience of these specialists enables them to understand everyone's concerns and anxieties and to maximise clients' chances of a successful outcome.

Top right: *Senior Partner Robert Turner welcomes Rob Kelly to the firm in September 2010.* ***Left:*** *Conveyancing team, L-R: Michelle Riordan, Diana Walker, Partner, Alison Withington and Ruth Walker.* ***Below:*** *Armitage Sykes Partners 2011, L-R: Robert M Turner LL.B (Head of Dept), Jeffrey Woodward LL.B, Philip Brewer M.A. (Oxon), Vivian J Lewis LL.B (Head of Dept), Ashley M Iredale LL.B.TEP (Head of Dept), Basharat Ali LL.B (Head of Dept), Diana J Walker LL.B (Head of Dept) and Martin Thompson LL.B.*

The Holset Turbocharger
An Iconic Engineering Brand

With facilities across the world including Europe, North America, South America, China and India, Cummins Turbo Technologies founded in St Andrew's Road, Huddersfield, is the world's leading designer of Holset turbochargers for commercial diesel engines.

In simple terms, a turbocharger comprises of a turbine and a compressor connected by a common shaft supported on a bearing system. The turbocharger converts waste energy from an engine's exhaust gases into compressed air, which it pushes into the engine. This allows the engine to burn more fuel, producing more power and improving the overall efficiency of the combustion process.

The company's early history in Huddersfield was modest. From 1948 to early 1952 the company traded as a division of W C Holmes manufacturing dampers and couplings. Premises comprised of a garage and a wooden hut. W C Holmes had become interested in the flexible couplings designed by Louis Croset in 1944.

During I948, W C Holmes obtained the manufacturing rights from Louis Croset, Paul Croset was persuaded to manage this new venture. He arrived in Huddersfield on 13 December, 1948. Paul Croset had earlier tested a viscous damper manufactured in the USA by Houdaille Industries. The tests showed that the Houdaille damper had a very short life. Paul designed a new damper using different materials. A patent was taken out and the manufacture and sale of viscous dampers began.

Paul Croset then heard that J & H McLaren of Leeds needed a reliable damper for their marine engine. He persuaded them to trial a prototype. A damper...and an order quickly followed. Rolls-Royce was another early customer ordering 50 viscous dampers for their new 6 cylinder engine.

Holset Engineering became a Limited Company on 29 March, 1952. The name derived from the family names of HOLmes and CroSET. Holset was a fully owned subsidiary of BHD Engineers Limited. Paul Croset was Holset's first Managing Director, DM Henshaw was the Chairman. Other board members were Louis Croset (Founder and Director), FB Holmes, H Whitely and P Rushworth (Secretary). At that time the Company still operated from the garage and the wooden hut and employed just 25 staff. Turnover was £4,500 but plans were in place to expand.

In August 1953, the first manufacturing bay was completed. By now the number of employees had grown to 42 and turnover had grown to £98,000. Competition, however, had been increasing since 1951 when Joseph Lucas had been given a

Top: *Paul Croset OBE, founder of Holset Engineering Co. Ltd.* ***Left:*** *The original wooden shed where Holset began, located in the steel scrapyard at the rear of W C Holmes offices off Turnbridge Road.* ***Above:*** *Ron Hesselden at the drawing boards inside the wooden hut.*

licence to manufacture Houdaille Dampers. Fortunately, Holset had foreseen this danger and Paul Croset took his first transatlantic flight to Buffalo, New York, USA to visit the President of Houdaille industries.

The visit was a success, each party agreed to respect each others patents and Joseph Lucas was instructed by the Ministry of Supply to grant Holset a sub-licence for Houdaille dampers.

Holset's interest in automotive radial-flow turbochargers began early in the 1950s. A licence was offered by Eberspächer of Germany which developed the first small air-cooled turbocharger for truck applications. Holset rejected this offer: however, Holset recognised the potential of turbochargers as a key future technology and began to research the technical and manufacturing processes of turbo charging by contacting Dr Alfred Büchi, the Swiss inventor of the first turbocharger.

The first exhaust-driven supercharger was developed by Dr Büchi between 1909 and 1912. An experimental turbo-charging plant had opened in Sulzer Bros Ltd, Winterthur, Switzerland in 1911. Büchi was Chief Engineer of the Sulzer Brothers Research Department, and in 1915 he proposed the first prototype of a turbocharged diesel engine, but his ideas gained little or no acceptance at that time.

It was to be 1925 before the first successful application of Büchi's work, on two German ships fitted with 2,000 hp turbocharged diesel engines. That success led to Büchi licensing many manufacturers in Europe, USA and Japan.

By the 1930s turbochargers with axial turbines were being used in marine, railcar and large stationary applications. In the following decade the advent of the aircraft gas turbine led to

Above: *Pictured from L-R are Louis Croset, Ron Hesselden, Brian Holmes, Paul Croset and Ernest Whitehead, all key figures in the early days of Holset.* ***Below:*** *The first office block opened in 1954 and (inset) the aftermath of the devastation left to the building by the fire in December 1967.*

major advances in materials technology and design: not least the development of improved heat resisting materials and precision casting techniques for high temperature materials - this in turn allowed the development of radial turbines and led to the use of radial flow 'turbos' on small automotive diesel engines.

Major engine producers such as Cummins, Volvo and Scania began experimenting with turbocharged engines for trucks using turbochargers supplied by Elliot and Eberspächer. These early designs were unsuccessful due to the large size of the turbocharger. German engineer, Kurt Beirer produces an innovative compact design that is taken up by Schwitzer Corporation, of Indianapolis. Pole position at the Indianapolis race in 1952 was won by a car powered by a turbocharged Cummins engine.

In 1954 Cummins offered a range of turbocharged engines, the VT12, six cylinder NT, NRTs and JTs. That same year Volvo offered its first turbocharged truck diesel, the TD96AS, rated at 185 bhp compared with the 150 bhp naturally aspirated D96AS.

By April 1954, a licence had been granted from Alfred Büchi for the manufacture and sale of exhaust gas-driven turbochargers in Huddersfield. Meanwhile the demand for dampers in West Germany was growing so quickly that there was no alternative but to grant a manufacturing licence to Carl Hasse & Werde of Berlin in order to meet demand.

In 1955 a licence agreement was granted with Sulzer Bros of Switzerland for the manufacture of viscous dampers for use on their own engines in the event of Holset being unable to supply.

A second manufacturing bay was completed during 1956 to accommodate the increased damper volumes. Initial contact had been made with Louis Schwitzer of the Schwitzer Corporation of Indianapolis, USA as early as 1952. After many negotiations, a licence agreement embracing the manufacture and sale of turbochargers and rubber dampers across Europe was signed in 1957. This agreement was a key milestone in the history of Holset taking the company firmly into the turbocharger business and making Holset the only company in the world capable of

Top left: *Inside Bay 1, manufacturing an inertia ring for the vibration damper for a Sulzer marine engine.* ***Above:*** *Craning an inertia ring for a 93 inch damper, one of the largest Holset made for a marine engine.* ***Below:*** *Paul Croset (far right) shows visitors the range of components manufactured in the former W C Holmes garage still adjoining the Technical Centre building in Huddersfield. Paul is holding a resilient gear.*

handling torsional vibration problems across the whole spectrum of internal combustion engines.

After the signing of the Schwitzer contract in 1957, extra manufacturing facilities were required. Bay 3 was primarily used for the machining assembly and testing of turbochargers. At the east end of the bay, Holset's first rubber manufacturing plant was set up for the production of inserts for rubber dampers and silicon 'O' ring seals for turbochargers. The rubber manufacturing plant was seen as a critical part of the business. It allowed Holset to control the specifications and the properties of the rubber to ensure that the highest quality rubber could be used on all products.

By 1959 the firm was employing 95 staff, whilst annual turnover had reached £664,000. The first production order for rubber dampers was obtained from the British Motor Corporation in November 1959. This was quickly followed by a succession of orders from Morris, Perkins, Rover, Vauxhall, Renault, Citroen and Beruet.

In 1964 the 25,000th turbocharger was produced. In honour of the occasion the turbocharger was presented to Louis Schwitzer jnr., President of the Schwitzer Corporation.

Early in the morning of 3 December, 1967, a fire destroyed both the production and administrative facilities at the Turnbridge site. Key records were lost: accounts, customer orders, production control data, planning, jig and tool records and component drawings. The latest IBM 1130 computer was also destroyed.

Employees, machine-tool manufacturers, sub-contractors and customers all co-ordinated to ensure that production lines were kept going and delivery dates met.

From the ashes of the fire, the Holset spirit of co-operation arose, enabling the Company to survive the disaster and re-build with confidence in the future.

Top left: *Coupling inner member manufactured for the main drive of a steel rolling mill.* ***Above:*** *Büchi components for the Büchi designed turbocharger.* ***Below:*** *A 1956 image of Bay 1 and Bay 2 and the first office block, designed by Shirley Holmes, daughter of Brian Holmes.*

That confidence has shown to have been more than justified, despite many changes which were in store for the firm.

In 1973 Hanson Trust Limited acquired the BHD Group, but the following year Cummins Engine Company, of USA purchased Holset from Hanson for £11 million.

Founded in Columbus, Indiana, in 1919 as Cummins Engine Company, named after its founder Clessie Lyle Cummins, the fledgling firm was among the first to see the commercial potential of an unproven engine technology invented two decades earlier by Rudolph Diesel.

After a decade of fits and starts, in 1933, the company released the Model H, a powerful engine for transportation that launched the company's most successful engine family. J. Irwin Miller, became general manager in 1934 and went on the lead the company to international prominence over the next four decades. By marketing high-quality products through a unique nationwide service organization, the company earned its first profit in 1937. Three years later, Cummins offered the industry's first 100,000-mile warranty.

By the 1950s, America had embarked on a massive interstate highway construction programme, with Cummins' engines powering much of the equipment that built those new roads and thousands of the trucks that began to roll down them. Truckers demanded economy, power, reliability, and durability, and Cummins responded. By the late 1950s, Cummins had sales of over $100 million and a commanding lead in the US market for heavy truck diesels.

As Cummins continued to grow its business in the United States, it also began looking beyond its traditional borders. Cummins opened its first foreign manufacturing facility in Shotts, Scotland, in 1956 and by the end of the 1960s Cummins had expanded its sales and service network to 2,500 dealers in 98 countries

The acquisition by Cummins in 1973 was the start of Holset's worldwide expansion. September 1978 brought the millionth turbocharger off the line and saw a turnover of £26 million. In 1983, Holset Aftermarket was established, with its headquarters in Huddersfield. Holset Aftermarket remanufactures and sells turbochargers and spare parts through a network of independent distributors worldwide.

An assembly plant was set up in Brazil, and a new manufacturing plant was built at Charleston, South Carolina, USA during the late 1980s. Joint ventures were established with the Tata Group of companies in India in 1994, and in 1995 in China with Wuxi Power.

Top left: *A view inside the factory in the 1950s.* ***Left:*** *Office block two constructed in 1969 enabling all administrative staff to be under one roof.* ***Above:*** *Testing in the 1980s.*

duty turbochargers to major Indian and overseas OEMs. This facility is built to world class standards and manufactures high quality turbochargers.

In 2010 the company launched a new range of turbochargers for the 2 to 5 litre diesel engine market

During 1996, the six millionth turbocharger rolled off the assembly line. The dampers and air compressors division of the business were now sold, along with the couplings division, allowing Holset to solely concentrate on the turbocharger market. Following on from this, 1997 saw the relocation of all manufacturing in the USA to two sites in Charleston and Columbus. In 1998, a brand new state-of-the-art Technical Centre was built on St. Andrew's Road in Huddersfield, and in 1999 Holset Aftermarket was relocated to the same site with new purpose-built facilities.

In 1998, Paul Croset OBE retired. He was awarded the OBE for his services to engineering in 1967.

On 29 March, 2002, Holset celebrated its 50th Anniversary as a Limited Company. HRH the Duke of Kent came to visit the Huddersfield site. Five founding members of Holset - Paul Croset, Bernard Ratcliffe, Tommy Dixon, Jeff Hall and Ron Hesselden were present to enjoy the special day. Six months later in October, 2002, at the Bonneville Salt Flats, Utah, Galebanks Engineering raced a Dodge Dakota with a Holset HY55V Variable Geometry Turbocharger. They broke the land speed record for a diesel pick-up truck with an amazing speed of 222mph.

In 2003, Holset's worldwide expansion continued with relocation to larger premises in China. 2004 saw an extension to the existing plant in India and in 2005 the announcement of a further plant in Charleston, USA.

Holset Turbochargers changed its name to Cummins Turbo Technologies on 2006 to align itself more closely with its parent company. That same year a new stand alone plant is opened in Charleston Palmetto, focusing on heavy-duty *VGT* (TM) turbocharger manufacturing serving North America and other global markets.

Cummins Inc. acquired the remaining equity ownership in its Indian joint venture; Tata Holset Limited, from the Tata Group of companies in 2007. Established in 2008, the Pithampur plant, India, supplies heavy-

In its 60 year history, Cummins Turbo Technologies has grown to become a US$1 billion company employing 3000 employees to design and produce 3 million turbochargers from nine plants worldwide. The Technical Centre houses the largest specialist turbocharger engineering team in the UK working to reduce emissions and improve fuel consumption on engines across the globe.

Top left: *In July 2010, Paul Croset toured the Huddersfield site.* ***Top right:*** *Viewing the Holset turbocharged Dodge Ram.* ***Above:*** *(l-r) Paul Croset, Jim Lyons, Ron Hesselden and Paul Ibbotson at the official opening of the Holset VGT (TM) line* ***Below:*** *Cummins Technical Centre, Huddersfield.*

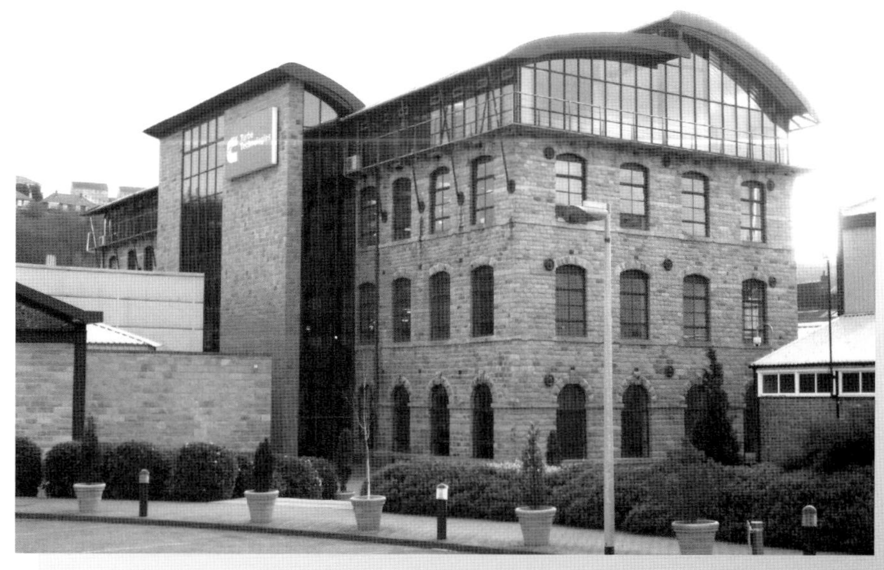

Myers Group - A Name Set in Stone

Two of our area's most prominent landmarks, Emley Moor Mast and Scammonden Bridge appear to have little in common. But there is an important link: Huddersfield's Myers Group, the concrete to quarrying consortium.

The Myers Group today comprises: Readymix Huddersfield Ltd, Naylor Myers Ltd, Johnsons Wellfield Quarries Ltd, Mobile Concrete Pumps, Mini Mix, Conveyormix, Boards Timber Merchants, Myers Build & DIY and Honley Skip Hire Ltd also known as HSH Skip Hire Ltd.

The Group offers so much more than just construction and building products. There is also focus on home interiors including kitchen design & plan, quality bathroom suites, tiles and wood flooring.

Based in Leeds Road, the Myers Group was born from an idea of Jack D Myers in the late 1950s as a natural development of the family's civil engineering business. That business was first incorporated in 1923 as Isaac Timmins Ltd, and it remains the parent company of the whole Myers Group.

Hervey Myers, grandfather of the current family directors, was a house builder from Mirfield. Most of his work was in the Dalton and Almondbury areas of Huddersfield building terraced and semi-detached properties. He also owned the Jesse Medley brickworks which were situated on Kilner Bank. Hervey, however, sold the brickworks to Elliots around 1940. In recent years the old Kilner Bank site has been landfilled and restored.

Above: *Jack Myers, founder of the Myers Group.* ***Bottom:*** *The Readymix - Huddersfield plant pictured in 1961.* ***Below inset:*** *Building the new Readymix plant.*

Though Hervey Myers was already established as a builder, Isaac Timmins was even better known. When Hervey acquired the Isaac Timmins business he chose to trade under the better known name. In the early days the business was based in Firth Street but around 1930 moved to Greenhead Avenue in Dalton.

Though today the Group has around 330 employees, the business was much smaller in the early days. At the time Hervey passed the firm to his only son Jack Douglas Myers in the early 1940s there were only some 30 or so employees. It says much for Hervey Myers that he was able to achieve so much during the 'Hungry Thirties' when every industry, not least the building trade, was in the doldrums.

The end of the great depression came in 1939 when Britain declared war on Germany. New factories were demanded, coastal defences and army camps were ordered. The outbreak of the Second World War set the scene for the hand-over from Hervey to Jack Myers, and a move from house building to infrastructure work. Jack had expected to be called up to serve in the armed forces but failed his medical; instead he spent the war years building runways and air defences in the East Riding and north Lincolnshire. Between 1939 and 1945 those airbases formed the launch pad for thousands of bombers and fighter planes which not only defended Britain's skies from Herman Goering's much-vaunted Luftwaffe, but in due course took the fight to Germany itself.

His experiences working on large building projects would serve Jack Myers well. In the post-war years civil engineering, roads and sewers became a mainstay of the business, working on district council projects in places such as Meltham, Kirkburton, Honley and Holmfirth.

In the late 1950s more ambitious projects were embarked upon working on larger road and sewer schemes for Huddersfield and Dewsbury councils.

Though the end of the First World War a generation earlier had been followed by a slump the period after the Second World War was unexpectedly one of continuing growth. Some parts of Britain had suffered enormous damage from German bombing, as a consequence a huge amount of building work needed to be done. A vast house building programme was promised by the Government and new roads, 'motorways' they were to be called, were to be built criss-crossing the country.

Jack Myers recognised there would be a need

Top left and above: *Preliminary work on the erection of a concrete shell for the new Emley Moor Mast in 1969.* ***Left:*** *Two 1960s Readymix lorries loading up.*

for a specialised supplier of ready mixed concrete and jointly established Readymix Huddersfield Ltd in 1959. The joint venture with Naylor, the pipemakers of Denby Dale, to produce Readymixed concrete led to plants being established in Huddersfield and Brighouse with a site plant later established on the M62 Pennine Contract for McAlpine. The M62 site plant would be subsequently transferred to Penistone.

Mobile Concrete Pumps was established in 1969 as one of the first concrete pumping firms to operate in the North of England.

Naylor Myers Building Supplies, which was formed in 1973, has ten depots and is the largest trading element within the Group.

Johnsons Wellfield Quarries, at Crosland Hill, was established in 1854 to satisfy the demand for building stone created by the industrial revolution. The business was acquired by the Readymix Huddersfield Group in 1979 and has continued to grow. The quarry would become the largest dimensional sandstone quarry and masonry works in Britain.

The early 1970s saw the Group's civil engineering activities being wound down with all efforts being concentrated on Readymix, Naylor Myers builders merchants and quarrying.

By the 1990s the business was being run entirely by the Myers family, culminating in June 1998 when Naylor interests were bought out and the Myers family achieved sole ownership and control of the Group.

The Group realised the need to offer ready mixed concrete which could be placed by conveyor into areas which were more difficult to reach, rather than releasing the concrete into an area where the customer would then have to move it by wheelbarrow. The conveyor arm at the rear of the mixer truck can reach into most locations

Conveyormix was introduced in July 2005 to complement the already successful Readymix Huddersfield, Mini Mix and Mobile Concrete Pumps. Conveyormix is specifically designed to deliver concrete into hard to reach areas previously inaccessible by the standard concrete mixer. An impressive telescopic remote controlled conveyor can reach up to 15 metres.

Together Readymix, Mini Mix, Conveyormix and Mobile Concrete Pumps provide a complete ready-mixed concrete placing service.

Boards Huddersfield, a traditional timber merchants on Canal Street, off Leeds Road, adjacent to Myers Group Head Office, was acquired in January 2006. Boards Timber Merchants supplies all types of timber and sheet materials; it complements

Top: *Johnsons Wellfield Quarries at Crosland Hill.* ***Left:*** *Naylor Myers Builders Merchants.* ***Above:*** *James and Katie Berry (right) proudly watch on as Ken Davy, Huddersfield Giants' Chairman, officially opens Myers Build & DIY in April 2011.*

Naylor Myers Builders Merchants by offering various timber products required for joinery projects associated with house building, including roof trusses, windows, doors, skirtings, architraves, flooring, fencing and more.

Myers Build & DIY, a one-stop-shop for building, renovation and DIY, was established in April 2011. The fourth generation of the Myers family, brother and sister James and Katie Berry, took full control of the launch of the new business under the Directors, brother and sister, John Myers and Jackie Berry.

Johnsons Wellfield Quarries has become the largest dimensional sandstone quarry in Britain. Hi-tec robot equipment has taken the place of traditional stone masons. Massive and continued investment in the most advanced stone-working machinery and quarry plant, together with commitment and determination to obtain new land reserves, has enabled Johnsons Wellfield to remain at the forefront of the UK stone industry. Johnsons is proud to be producing award winning natural stone of the very highest quality from the state of the art production facility at Crosland Hill.

Crosland Hill Yorkstone has been utilised locally and throughout the country for many prestigious projects including: The regeneration of St George's Square, Huddersfield, Huddersfield University Creative Arts Building, Huddersfield University Business School, Wm Morrisons' Headquarters, Bradford, Tudor Square, Sheffield, Sheaf Square, Sheffield, Paternoster Square, London, the Tower of London and the V&A Museum London.

Johnsons Wellfield sees 'sustainability' as a fundamental guiding principal which shapes the thinking behind how it conducts the business and plans for the future. Continued investment in energy efficient stone processing technologies and development of 'Natural Stone Engineering' techniques ensure that the objective standards set in quality and sustainable materials sourcing are clearly met. An 'open door policy' for clients and customers offers not only a glimpse into the future of the industry but also reassurance that the Crosland Hill mineral will be available for generations to come.

The Group looks to the future with optimism, continuing to invest in its branch network, manufacturing facilities and transport fleet. These investments provide the reliability and efficiencies needed to meet ever increasing levels of customer expectation.

Today, the fourth generation of the Myers family, James and Katie Berry, are actively involved in continuing the family business. They can look back with pride at their family's contribution to such prestigious local projects as the M62 Scammonden Bridge and dam, Kingsgate shopping centre, the Galpharm Stadium, the Emley Moor mast and Winscar reservoir, with many more, equally prestigious projects yet to come.

Left: *One of the company's high-tech robots in operation at Johnsons Wellfield.* ***Top left and below:*** *Recent natural stone supply projects by Johnsons Wellfield – St George's Square, (top left) and Huddersfield University Creative Arts Building.*

J B Schofield & Sons

Six Generations of Recycling

Long before recycling was heard of, the Schofield family were earning a living doing exactly that: woollen waste, leather belting, wooden bobbins, anything that the textile industry could reuse. Today, J B Schofield & Sons Ltd is still at it.

Woollen waste dealer James Schofield was born in 1828. In 1876 he and his wife Elizabeth bought land and property at Greenhead, Linthwaite. James died in 1892 with the property passing to his wife. Upon her death in 1908 Joe Benjamin (J B) Schofield one of James' four children paid £700 for the property and three acres of land and the business of J B Schofield was born, by now dealing in scrap metal. The business is therefore even older than the 'established 1912' which appeared on the firm's vehicles.

Joe Schofield had four sons, two of whom, Norman and Stanley, took the opportunity in 1920 to buy another eight acres of land for £410. In 1941 Norman paid £800 to buy the rest of the family's share in the property at Greenhead.

In 1933, some 13 years after Joe's death, the first diesel-engined vehicle came along, YG8732, a Morris commercial. By 1954 Norman had scraped the money together to buy the company's first new vehicle, a Perkins P6-engined Dodge 5-tonner. Norman also bought the business of W Oldcorn from his friend William 'Bill' Oldcorn. Involved in coal and general haulage W Oldcorn still trades from the same office as J B Schofield.

Norman's death at the age of 67 in 1964 led to Carl and younger brother George taking over the business. The brothers set about expanding, forming J B Schofield & Sons Ltd.

Larger vehicles from Foden, the best premium vehicle of that era, was the chosen marque. A new crane with an electro magnet for handling the ferrous scrap metal, crawler excavators, wheeled loaders and crawler cranes were all acquired, with demolition and plant hire were now being undertaken.

Top left: *Norman Schofield and wife Winnifred.* ***Above:*** *Norman, Stanley and young Carl Schofield in 1936* ***Below:*** *Greenhead in 1960.*

During the 1960s in the Colne Valley rows of cottages were being condemned keeping the demolition equipment busy. Industrial demolition sites were also providing scrap metal for the scrap processing side of the business. Many new houses were being built from the stone and wood reclaimed.

Back in the scrapyard at Greenhead, redundant machinery from the textile industry was being processed into feedstock for local foundries and Sheffield's steelworks.

Further afield, Skinningrove's famous steelworks in the North East was a regular destination by both day and night.

Another regular customer was the Dick Lane foundry of English Electric in Bradford, where Carl struck up a friendship with Harry Wilkinson, the purchasing manager. English Electric was to become the bedrock of Schofield's ferrous scrap metal business during the 1970s and 80s.

The cupolas at Dick Lane needed up to 800 tonnes a month of low phosphorous cast iron, this 'grade 17' cast iron was to be Schofield's speciality. Carl persuaded Harry Wilkinson to accept grade 17 cast iron 'skull' broken small and blended with the other broken castings, brake drums and engines. Skull could be bought cheaper, therefore raising the profit margin on the whole load. On top of this the breaking process was refined, a purpose-made breaking pit with thick steel bedded in tarmac meant that even in the depths of winter Schofield's cast iron was clean. Most other merchants were breaking in filthy conditions; a larger 1.25 tonne steel breaking ball, a crane with a 40ft jib meant that they could break material that others couldn't touch.

All incoming materials were analysed, checking for correct carbon, silicon and phosphorous levels; in fact up to 16 elements were checked. This extra information meant that Schofield's could more accurately blend the cast iron mix. By now there were separating and screening plants too, fed by Schofield's dragline and loading shovels separating the metal runnings from foundry sand, and a waste skip service taking waste to landfill sites. This was all to end in 1990 with the closure of the foundry.

The next generation of Schofields had joined the business during the 1970s: Carl's eldest son Mark and George's sons Andrew, Richard and Michael.

Now came local authority work. Carl had had a chance meeting with the area engineer for the newly formed West Yorkshire Metropolitan Council, Keith Dwyer. Carl was invited to tender for hire work including winter road maintenance, gritting and snow ploughing. It became Carl's passion. By 1980 almost every piece of equipment Schofield's owned had

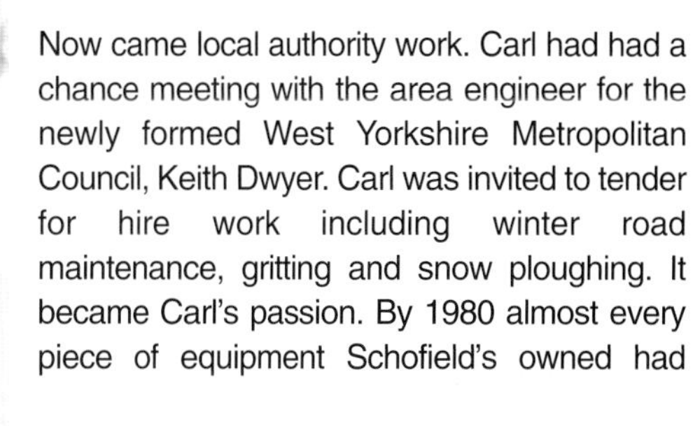

Top left: *W Oldcorn Ltd bought by Norman Schofield still operates from the same offices as J B Schofield today.* ***Left:*** *A Schofield crawler shovel and inset a snowplough snow clearing.* ***Above:*** *Carl Schofield pictured in the 1970s on board one of the company gritters.*

been adapted to move snow: 16 bulk gritters, tippers with ploughs, crawler shovels, JCBs, everything was utilised, working to keep the trans-Pennine passes open.

Many of Schofield's gritters were unique, built and modified in their own workshops, sandblasted and sprayed by Mark with rust preventative paint. Most of the workforce enjoyed doing it. There were occasions, however, when with his diesel frozen and waxy, (yes diesel does freeze) salt frozen solid, hands and feet colder still, a driver might long to be home in bed.

For Carl one of the problems with gritting was that his stocks of cast iron, pre-broken ready for delivery, would dwindle whilst he was out in his snowplough. To counter that risk, year on year the piles grew bigger and the roadways around the site narrower; by the time Dick Lane foundry closed there was enough stock for two years melting left.

Around 2007 Mark took the decision not to tender for the gritting contract again. Compliance with the rules and regulations surrounding the contract was compromising the running of the metal processing and delivery side of things. Chaotic road conditions on the west side of Huddersfield led to the formation of a 'Bring back Schofield' facebook page. A decision by Mark to launch a website created one of the most informative metal recycling sites on the web. Photos of historic vehicles, new vehicles and extreme snow conditions are all included at www.jbschofieldandsons.co.uk

Schofield's smartly kept high-spec Fodens had been a familiar sight on the northern roads for over 40 years; these vehicles, along with the gritters, have been featured in several heritage commercial magazine articles, with words and photographs supplied from keen amateur photographer Mark's massive archive.

The Greenhead site has seen much modernisation over the years, a non-ferrous sorting shop, a four-bay vehicle workshop, tarmac roadways, new weighbridge, site concrete, drainage, the introduction of strict health and safety rules and environmental legislation, and IT systems; each in its turn affecting the working lives of the Schofield family.

Mark's two sons, another Carl and John (another JB), established themselves in the family business. Schofield's legendary mountains of scrap seemed never to change, though much of the incoming material is processed and loaded for export the same day, only the higher grade foundry material being stockpiled.

Sadly, the smartly-presented Foden trucks are a thing of the past. The demise of the UK truckmaker means that vehicles are now being sourced from Germany.

The new millennium has seen a steady shift towards trading in Non Ferrous Metals like copper and brass. Mark's eldest daughter Leigh has joined the business and is making her mark in the office,

Top: *One of Schofield's Foden dumpertrucks.* ***Left:*** *Unloading scrap with a crane magnet in the mid-1980s.* ***Above:*** *At work with the Sennebogen scrap handling machine, 2008.*

having spent a large part of her childhood in the scrapyard and its vehicles. And Elizabeth, Leigh's younger sister, has studied accountancy since school, a valued skill in the family business. Schofield's appetite for the high grade foundry feed, that is its stock in trade, means that material is now sourced from as far north as Edinburgh and as far south as London.

Although the recession of 2008 hit hard, the policy of retaining profits in the business meant that Schofield could weather the storm, and crucially invest in new equipment, taking advantage of competitive deals. New vehicles are once again delivering quality foundry feed throughout the country.

The sad death of Carl's younger brother George after a short illness has led to a change in the ownership of shares in the business. George's youngest son Michael wanted to leave to follow a new career; this in turn led to Michael's brothers Andrew and Richard selling their shares too. The ownership of the business, has, yet again, followed one branch of the family. A new generation of Schofields now looks back with fondness and pride at the company's rich and varied history, whilst looking forward to the future with keen anticipation.

***Top:** Easy does it now! A huge scrap tanker arrives at Greenhead in July 2009. **Left:** Schofield's MAN Hookloader. **Below:** The Greenhead yard with Schofield's Sennebogens and a MAN flatbed in view.*

W T Johnson & Sons - The Finishing Touch

WT Johnson & Sons Ltd, the Huddersfield company based at Bankfield Mills, Moldgreen, produces world-class finishes for woollen and worsted cloth. It was founded in 1910 when Walter Thomas Johnson set up in business in premises on Wakefield Road. He had decided to branch out with his own company, aged about 50 years, after serving as Foreman Finisher at Glendinning's.

No-one has ever been able to explain satisfactorily exactly why in the 17th century the wool trade suddenly began to dominate in our part of Britain. England had already had a thriving woollen industry for centuries, but it was based in Yorkshire's East Riding, East Anglia and Somerset. There were no new technical innovations at the time which might explain the phenomenal growth of weaving in the West Riding of Yorkshire. Some suggest that it was demand for cloth to make uniforms for the armies then fighting all over Europe which stimulated new demands on British weavers. Others suggest that the enclosure of common land drove local smallholders to find something else to do. Still others point to the trade guilds, early trade unions, which in other parts of the country restricted recruitment to the weaving trade. These ancient institutions did not operate strongly in the Pennine valleys, so allowing the trade to grow here at a dramatic pace. These provided the motive and the opportunity. The means were wool and water. By the 18th century, however, wool was being imported into the Colne Valley from far and wide to keep up with its looms

One of the most important elements in the historical success of the Yorkshire woollen industry has been the soft West Yorkshire water. Water flowing down steep valleys or kept back in mill ponds could be used to drive power looms. But equally importantly the soft water made it easy to wash wool and finish cloth - a critical part of the whole process.

Top left: *Founder, Walter Johnson.* ***Above:*** *Washing machines used by the company in the early days.* ***Below:*** *Cropping machines.*

W T Johnson thought it would be a great advantage to have its own water supply on site brought directly from a well, for two reasons: firstly it would not have to pay the water company to supply it, therefore minimising costs and, secondly, the water would be pure, making it ideal for washing the fabric. The Manchester firm of drilling experts, Thomas Matthews felt sure that water would be found on the site. Boring commenced in the late 1930s and the hole reached the depth of about 300 feet which was the standard well depth, but there was no water. Undaunted, Matthews kept drilling (and invoicing Johnson's accordingly). When the hole had reached a depth of 1,000 feet, 'WT' felt that further expenditure could not be justified on what seemed to be a fruitless project. However, Rex Matthews, who was supervising the operation, was so unshakeably convinced that water would be found that he said he would go on drilling and allow 'WT' to pay him back when he could. Rex's confidence was not misplaced and water was indeed struck - at a depth of more than 1,500 feet (it is believed to be the deepest well in Yorkshire). The firm has reaped the benefit of its own uncontaminated free water supply since 1940 when the associated pipework was laid down.

When Walter Johnson took his son, Walter Marshall Johnson ('WM'), into partnership with him this was a complete change of direction for the younger Walter who had only recently passed his Civil Service exams. Today, Walter Thomas's great-grandsons are continuing the family tradition, the fourth generation to be involved in the business.

The two Walters, father and son, worked together for the first few years, but later Walter senior's other sons, Tom and Frank, joined them. The third generation into the business were Walter

Marshall's son Peter and Frank's son David. The tradition is that all family members are fully acquainted with each and every part of the business.

Top: *The Scouring Department.* ***Above left:*** *The original Bankfield Mills - built in 1829 and the home of WT Johnson since 1910. The building is still in use today within the current WT Johnson & Sons site.* ***Above:*** *Sons of the founder. Pictured L-R are Walter Marshall, Tom and Frank.*

Although over the years some Johnsons have inevitably spent more time on one area than another, they are all conversant with the technical side of things and control what is happening in the workshop and with their customers.

Many difficulties had to be overcome down the years. One of the first hurdles to be surmounted by the infant Johnson firm was to repay a personal loan granted by a Mr Sykes of Norwood Green. He is also believed to have owned the premises occupied by the firm. Today the firm is still operating from the same address in Wakefield Road, Huddersfield, but the site has seen significant expansion and development over the years.

Much of this development took place in the 1950s when land adjacent to the site which had previously been Huddersfield Corporation allotments was acquired for new building work - indeed they would have liked more, but this was not made available to the company.

In the 18th and 19th centuries, in the early days of the Colne Valley's woollen industry, work was carried out by firms which did everything, starting with the raw wool from the sheep, through spinning, weaving, dyeing and finishing. As time went on, however, some firms started to specialise on one process, Johnson's was one of them. In the 1970s Johnson's took over Tom Lees & Co, Dyers from Honley, renaming the company DP Dyers Ltd. This added specialist piece dying to their finishing business. Concentrating on a specific area gave a number of advantages - they were able to build up expertise in that particular process and were able to direct their resources into the best available machinery for the job.

Some firms, like Crowther's, continued to offer the entire range of processes, but they were in decline. Johnson's chose to specialise in finishing, and invested accordingly. Though the equipment available for carrying out the finishing process has changed over time as technology has brought new levels of accuracy and complexity to the procedure, the original raison d'etre of the company remains the same as it was during World War I, namely to take woollen cloth as it comes straight from the loom and wash it (usually with soap and water), dry it and press it using the most up-to-date machinery.

A great number of variations are now possible in each of these three stages of the finishing process. This enables Johnson's to add real value to the fabric it finishes and become an important contributor to the creation of new fabrics. The quality and uniformity of the finish is also of paramount importance. Today's customers demand repeatable finishes due to the popularity of 'mix and match' clothing - items of an outfit bought separately need to look good together and be a genuine match.

It is a point of pride in the company that it is a supplier of a process which meets important 'green' criteria: no detergents or synthetic additives are used in the

***Top left:** Third generation, David (left) and Peter Johnson, Chairman. **Left:** Ekofast - the cornerstone of many of W T Johnson & Sons' finishes. The high temperature continuous setting giving permanent softness and stability with 100% continuity. The company's two machines are unique, having been developed from the original. **Above:** Jet Scour - this ground breaking machine allows scouring and softening of the most delicate of fabrics.*

processes and this gives the company a leading edge in today's marketing climate where 'natural' and 'sustainable' are coveted accolades. WT Johnson & Sons remains confident in its continuing ability to stay ahead of the competition, not just in its commitment to technology and profitability but also in its environmental credentials.

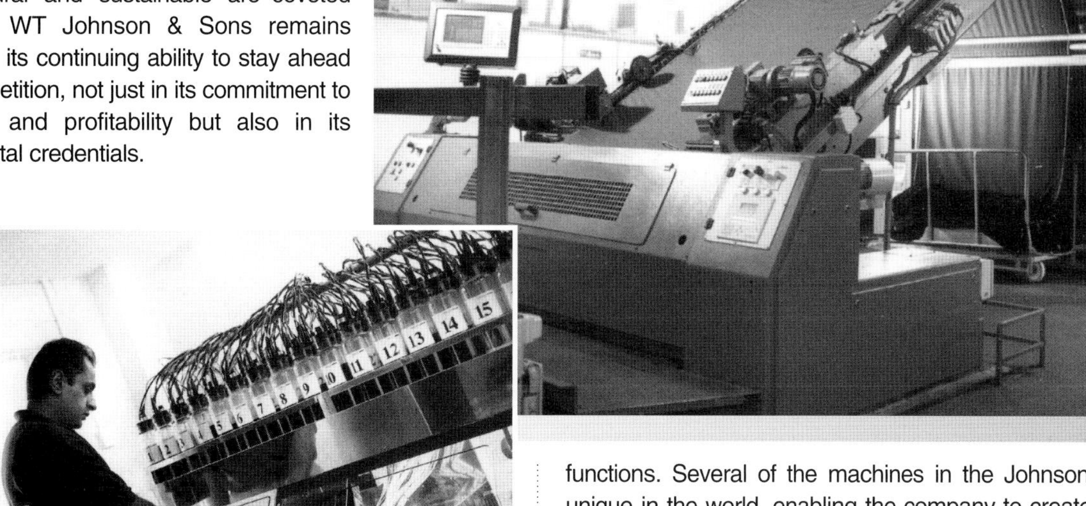

To remain in business all companies need to stay ahead of their competitors, and this is particularly so when the industry concerned is in decline, as is the case with the woollen industry. Many local mills are now derelict. It is a testament to the quality of the Johnson treatments that the company is still in business in this highly competitive international market. It is not only local firms which represent rival bidders for available work, but also developing countries which have significantly lower labour costs as well as Italian companies in the same field.

The specialist skills of Johnson's master textile finishers have been passed down through the generations. Walter Marshall 'WM' Johnson's son Peter has guided the technical development of the firm for over 50 years. Today his sons Paul and Dan are managing the business. One of Peter's key skills has been in refining the existing plant technology and creating innovative new machinery to perform highly specific finishing functions. Several of the machines in the Johnson's mill are unique in the world, enabling the company to create bespoke, high quality finishes on an ever increasing range of fabrics.

Today the company employs over 90 people, providing a product which is the best in the business - a result of a century of Johnson expertise and consistently investing in the best staff and equipment available.

Top left: *Colour Laboratory - this contains a computerised match prediction system that measures colour and then calculates the required recipe. The lab dyeing machine provides for the accurate dispensing of dye for producing small shade cuttings for customer shade cards or as trials prior to bulk dyeings.* ***Top right:*** *Drying - a combination of state of the art mechanical water removal and gas fired drying allows for maximum machine efficiencies. In addition, fabric dimensions and residual moisture levels can be precisely controlled.* ***Left:*** *Fine Tailoring - W T Johnson & Sons are proud to provide the very finest quality finished fabrics used by talented tailors to produce the most highly prized made-to-measure suits in the world.* ***Above:*** *Paul Johnson, Managing Director (left) and Dan Johnson, Director.*

Garrards

Huddersfield's Oldest Timber Company

Garrards is the oldest timber merchants in Huddersfield; it is a firm with a long-established and well-earned reputation as a small, caring and friendly business. Founded a century ago, these days it has become a national business, selling from its branches and the internet to customers nationwide.

The firm has its own timber mill, with excellent machining facilities; it can offer specialised machining to match any existing pattern or special requirements. Garrards also keeps a wide range of machined items always in stock, in both softwood and hardwood.

Stanley Garrard had already been in the timber business since 1905 when the present firm was set up in 1917 as a partnership between himself and a Mr Eastwood.

At their premises in Great Northern Street, where the company still flourishes today, the partnership's original activity was the construction of wooden ammunition boxes for use in the Great War, then in its third year. Mr Eastwood's connection with the business, however, lasted only three or four years, and there is no subsequent record of his activities.

Above: *A Garrards float taking part in a 1950s parade honouring the efforts of the soldiers in the First World War.* ***Below:*** *Founder Stanley Garrard and his wife with cause for celebration raise their glass.*

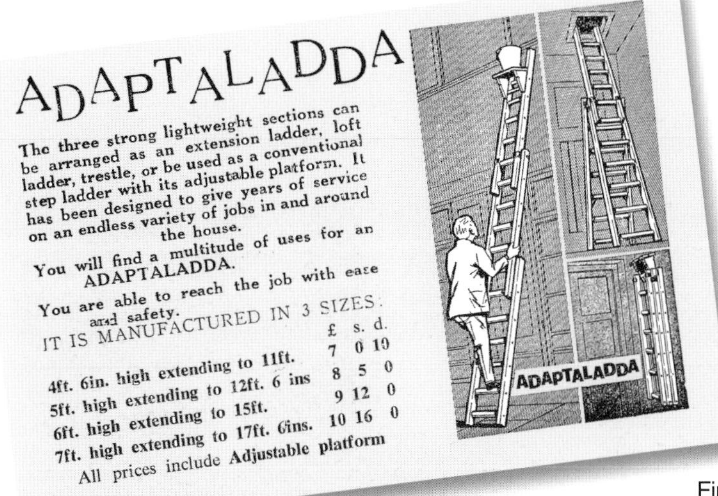

Stanley Garrard on the other hand stayed with the firm until his well-earned retirement, which he spent on the Isle of Man. On Stanley's retirement the business was taken over by his son Geoffrey. Under Geoffrey Garrard's leadership the timber business continued to grow.

With the advent of the Second World War in 1939 the company returned to its original purpose and function, making packing cases for ammunition. Like all firms, they lost some of their men to service in the armed services but nevertheless continued working; meanwhile, their workforce in the office began to contain more women, something of a novelty in those days when the timber trade was an exclusively male preserve.

By this time Derek Stott was managing director, and it was Derek who held the fort when Geoffrey Garrard died in a tragic drowning accident. Geoffrey's favourite form of relaxation had been sailing his boat, which he kept on Lake Windermere. He and his family had been on holiday there when the tragedy occurred.

The Garrards had four children, but the eldest was only 15. In the absence of a suitable family member to take immediate control Derek Stott ran the business for them.

However, it was very soon discovered that heavy death duties were going to make for difficult times for the Garrard family. Derek Stott therefore bought the Garrards out and went on running the business as its owner, though keeping the company name unchanged.

But if Derek Stott thought life might be easy in future he was very much mistaken. Shortly after Derek bought the firm it suffered a setback in the form of a serious fire.

Fire is the constant fear in every timber yard. Many tons of wood stacked many feet high can quickly become a raging inferno once flames get hold.

The blaze occurred on a night when the Huddersfield Fire Brigade had to deal with four fires in two hours. Several thousand pounds worth of damage was caused to the firm's hardwood store and its contents.

Delayed by a small fire at Scarbottom Mills in Milnsbridge, the firemen arrived to find flames already leaping through the roof. Despite the severe damage the fire was prevented by the fire crews from spreading to the firm's other timber stores.

Derek Stott had been in charge for only three or four years when he too died suddenly on holiday. As a consequence, from the late 1970s, the firm belonged to Derek's widow Margaret, and was run by its managing director Melvyn Clelland.

Top left: *A page from the company's DIY catalogue from 1969. At the time their most expensive ladder cost nearly £11.* ***Left:*** *Geoffrey Garrard and his wife pictured in the early 1960s.* ***Below:*** *Derek Stott surveys the damage to the hard timber store the morning after the disastrous fire.*

Garrards seldom sees the goods that its containers are to be used for. Its customers specify the dimensions and materials required and the company delivers the finished containers.

Often they go that extra mile to help clients. For example, when the United States was taking military action in Libya in the early 1970s and there was an embargo on exports there from the UK, Garrards offered storage facilities to one of its customers. The client's business was the production of desalination plants to the Middle East and their equipment had overflowed their own storage space as they waited for the government embargo to be lifted.

Meanwhile, although Garrards has remained in its premises at Great Northern Street for all its nine decades, as the company's business has grown, it has acquired and moved into neighbouring buildings.

When Garrards took over the premises of boiler company Alan Knight the building had to be cleared of huge pieces of equipment, including whole boilers and steam rollers, before the place could be demolished and completely rebuilt. A further plot of land, which had contained 50 houses, was cleared by the Council before the company acquired it.

The managing director's least pleasant experience came in 1978 when, accompanied by a policeman and his dog, they found the Yorkshire Ripper's 13th victim on-site.

As is fitting for the oldest timber company in Huddersfield, Garrards has earned customer satisfaction through applying skilled craftsmanship to good quality materials according to each individual customer's requirements.

Garrards has worked chiefly with timber and plywood to make crates, cases and pallets of any size a customer requires. However an increasingly important aspect of the business is selling DIY equipment to Huddersfield householders.

An in-house Trade Centre has been introduced to help provide all the accessories any individual or company may need to perform specific joinery and wood working jobs.

The Trade Centre stocks products from many of the leading brand names including Dewalt, Stanley, BlackFriar, Brummer, Union, Chubb, Vitrex, Bond-It and many more.

Softwoods, Hardwoods, Sheet Material, Doors, Stairparts, Worktops, Windows, Loft Ladders, Flooring, Fencing, Pineboard, MFC, Building Materials and Decking are all now on offer. A large range of both soft and hard woods are always kept in stock including a variety of specialist woods, such as maple, cherry maple, oak, sapele and many more that the sawmill can cut to measure.

Garrards normally selects all its timbers for stock itself, direct from the quay. That way the company can assure the quality of its timber. The company also supplies direct from the quay should clients require full loads, or it can obtain smaller amounts

Top left: *A Garrrards flatbed.* ***Above:*** *The entrance to Garrards' Joinery Centre and Showroom.* ***Left:*** *Garrards exhibition stand at the Northern Homebuilding & Renovation Show in Harrogate in 2010.*

of any size or quality of timber, subject to availability, to suit requirements.

Deliveries are made using the firm's own vehicles, and new wagons have increased load capacity significantly.

Transport has not been the only investment: a new office extension has been built, there have been improvements to a new joinery centre, new products have been introduced such as heavy building materials, and there has also been significant expenditure on new woodworking machines at the firm's production mill.

Simon Chapman, Garrards general manager says: "The heavy products are now on sale in addition to probably Huddersfield's most comprehensive timber range which includes decking products, anti-slip decking, brand new q-deck lyptus hardwood decking, an extensive choice of fencing and other hard landscaping products for the spring and summer gardener. Although many of our customers are local tradesmen, Garrards always welcomes local homeowners and keen DIY enthusiasts looking for top quality timber products for their home.

If you're looking to improve your garden and outdoor area, then come and look at the extensive range of fencing, landscaping and decking products, along with all the ancillary fixtures and fittings to complete the look."

Transforming your garden can be relatively easy with a little help from Garrards. Take a look at the decking display area to see what's available".

Simon adds "Despite constantly moving forward, we still work to traditional values and put great emphasis on personal service, top quality excellent products and good value for money. Any homeowners visiting Garrards always receive expert help and advice in choosing their products and carrying out their home improvements. People are always surprised when they come here at how much help and expert knowledge is available."

Most recently a new hardwood shed has helped make Garrards into one of the largest timber merchants in the region, stocking hardwoods from all over the world.

Through new initiatives and investment Garrards is now the busiest it has ever been. Each year sets a new record.

Proud of their heritage, and proud to be independent, Garrards' progressive ownership, management and 28 staff are now set to start their second century of excellence in the timber trade.

Top: *Garrrards' Jumbo Valmar sideloader.* ***Left:*** *Simon Chapman, General Manager.* ***Below:*** *Garrards Timber Merchants' Great Northern Street premises, 2011.*

Bower Roebuck - Tradition & Technology

The Royal Wedding of 2011 was an opportunity for every guest to don their finest outfits for the occasion. And few looked more dashingly dressed than England's best known footballer David Beckham. Though David's suit may have been designed in the USA and tailored in Italy the real secret was in the cloth – material specially commissioned from the famous local firm of Bower Roebuck.

The technological advances made in the last few decades have seen an extraordinary change in the textile industry. At Glendale Mills, in New Mill, Huddersfield, however, they have not forgotten their traditional craftsmanship in the race to use new technology.

New Mill, the home of Bower Roebuck, takes its name from the mill built there in 1315, when local corn production exceeded the capacity of the mill at nearby Holmfirth. The dissolution of the monasteries broke the monopoly on milling in 1536, at which time the abundant energy of the millstream was harnessed to drive cloth fulling machines for the first time, and thus the textile industry of the Holme Valley was born.

During the 18th and 19th centuries, each consecutive technological advance brought its own dramatic social and financial changes. In 1899, the mill was renamed Glendale Mills by its owners, Messrs Bower and Roebuck.

Since then the ubiquitous spread of central heating, air conditioning and warm cars during the last 100 years or so has meant that lighter more fluid cloths have developed and the heavy thick materials which once protected the wearer in drafty old buildings and ice cold carriages have gradually lost prominence. Back then it would have been considered extraordinary to create a cloth of less that 400 gms (grams per linear metre) in weight, yet now Bower Roebuck rarely produces cloth over 300 gms, and can produce down to as little as 160 gms if required.

Above: *The sign of quality - Bower Roebuck's ticket and seal.* ***Below:*** *A bird's eye view of Bower Roebuck and the village of New Mill.*

Much else has changed too. When the company was first formed its market was restricted to Britain and limited parts of Europe. Delivery took several months and was often at the mercy of the sea and poor weather. Even so the company has always had an export market to wherever there has been a demand for quality British cloth. Today the firm operates in a global market, its traditional markets have expanded and been augmented, whilst technological advances make production, transport and communication faster ever day.

As part of the Scabal Group since 1973, the firm's focus on quality has consistently led to expansion, investment and prosperity.

Soon after the textile industry's benchmarks of Super 80s and Super 100s classifications were introduced, Scabal and Bower Roebuck took the initiative. In the early 1970s it became the first company to manufacture cloth classified as Super 120s, approximately one micron finer than the first Super 100s. A decade later, it again led the field by manufacturing the first Super 150s quality cloth, using 15.3 micron wool. These are now international standards of quality and excellence. Even these standards are now surpassed at Bower Roebuck, using yarn counts and wool microns that were previously thought to be beyond technology.

Towards the end of the 20th century the mill was the first to weave cloth classified as Super 180s and Super 200s.

Apart from the ultrafine all-wool qualities the company also produces cashmere blends, silk blends and 100% cashmere suiting fabrics - specialist products only a few companies in the UK or Italy would even attempt.

Bower Roebuck has been at the forefront of technological advancement over the centuries. As long ago as 1779, the company was the first to install mechanised wool carding machines. This tradition has continued into the modern era with the introduction of the first computerised design sample looms, effectively bringing the method of producing design ranges and

Top: *New machinery being lifted into Bower Roebuck in 1905.* ***Above:*** *A former early 20th century weaving machine of Bower Roebuck.*

samples forward by some 50 years. Over recent years, Bower Roebuck has invested several million pounds in a modernisation programme, installing the latest Dornier rapier looms and sophisticated computer equipment.

Theoretically, if someone bought the machinery and computer systems in use at Bower Roebuck and purchased the same raw materials, they could produce the same high quality cloth - but not in practice. They would lack the experience and dedication of the firm's workforce and the years of experience of its design team.

The technological advances are inherently connected to the desire to constantly improve the quality or product. The company's values and standards transcend technology and hark back to a tradition of craftsmanship, a time when the hand, eye and judgment, still Bower Roebuck's most valued tools, worked together unaided to produce good, honest cloth. They make all the difference.

Bower Roebuck's parent company, Scabal SA, was a family business, started in 1938 in Brussels, where the head office is still located. The name Scabal comes from the company's European initials, 'Société Commerciale Anglo-Belgo-Allemande et Luxembourgeoise'.

In addition to the Huddersfield manufacturing business, Scabal has a garment factory in Germany and retail outlets around the world, embracing Japan, Hong Kong, the United States, Russia and major European cities - including a flagship store in London's Savile Row.

It is the extraordinary quality and imaginative genius of its fabrics that continue to drive Scabal's success. The first company to introduce qualities such as Super 120s,150s, 180s and 200s it has also launched a series of ground-breaking cloths which have redefined the meaning of luxury in the increasingly high value world of men's suitings. Such qualities include Diamond Chip, the first cloth ever produced containing diamond fragments; Lapis Lazuli; and Summit, the ultimate in fine micron worsted fabric.

The Spanish painter Salvador Dali was commissioned by Scabal in 1971 to paint several pictures for the company to depict the artist's interpretation of what clothes would look like at the turn of the century. These continue to inspire fabric collections which together with the designers from Bower Roebuck are created and manufactured in Huddersfield, along with the other unique fabrics.

Savile Clifford, a name with historical links with Bower Roebuck was formed by the Scabal Group in 2005 to manufacture fine fabrics for suitings and jacketings in wool and alluring blends for younger professionals.

Top left and above: *Computer aided sample warping and weaving.* ***Left:*** *The newest Rapier production looms.*

The company targets the better end of the medium and higher price market for ready-to-wear worsteds and offers a contemporary take on the tradition and culture that are unique to English cloths. Using the administration, manufacturing and quality excellence of Bower Roebuck, Savile Clifford operates entirely independently from its sister company with respect to design development, sales and customer base.

In the few years that it has been in existence its collections and reputation have been well established with the designer houses and brand names in Europe and the Far East. Consequently its contribution to the success and future of Bower Roebuck is significant.

It is another example of Scabal's ongoing development and investment to expand its business and underlines the group's commitment to production in Europe and in the UK in particular.

Meanwhile, even disaster has been turned to triumph at Bower Roebuck. In July 2002 flash flooding in the area resulted in the mill being inundated with water one metre deep running through the mill. The consequence was complete closure of on-site production for six months whilst £4 millions worth of new machinery was commissioned and installed making Bower Roebuck one of the most modern textile manufacturers in the world, employing over 70 local workers. That investment continued in 2008 when the firm installed a new warping machine, which is still the only one of its kind in the UK.

Today, a wealth of meticulously detailed design archives, and huge bound books of catalogued samples, trace the evolution of more than a century of design at Bower Roebuck. Cloth from hundreds of collections is represented, as well as technical specifications and other indispensable information. It is common to see 'retro' looks emerging, reflecting classic designs from a previous decade, with themes reinterpreted in contemporary cloth. It is both a mark of continuity, and a source of

reassurance, that in the same way that the cloth designed today has often been inspired by the past, so in turn today's designs will one day become the inspiration for cloth of the future.

From princes of industry to princes of the realm, from pop stars, to football stars, Bower Roebuck makes cloth to suit them all.

Top left: *Customised name list woven on fabric.* ***Left:*** *Skilled mending of fabric.* ***Above:*** *A century of archived samples.* ***Below:*** *A view of the weaving shed.*

Kirklees College - Past, Present and Future

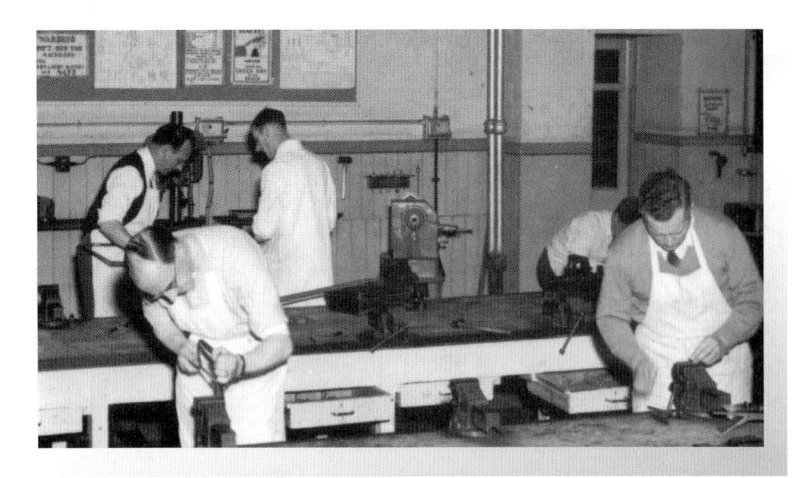

Kirklees College has some big ambitions. And if you've driven along Manchester Road you'll have seen one of those ambitions coming to life. Scheduled to open in September 2012, the college's brand new state-of-the-art campus for its learners, in the shape of the Huddersfield Centre, Waterfront Quarter was several years in the planning.

Occupying the triangular site bounded by Manchester Road, Chapel Hill and the River Colne, the centre will form part of a joint venture between Yorkshire Forward and Kirklees Council.

The project will also open up the Huddersfield Narrow Canal, which runs under the site, to create an attractive waterway, which will also provide cooling water for the college building. For the first time in living memory the public will be able to access the river and canalside footpaths in this part of Huddersfield.

The origin of Further Education in Huddersfield can be traced back to 1825 with the foundation of the Huddersfield Scientific and Mechanics Institute.

The Mechanics Institute moved to premises on Queen Street South in 1884. It became a Technical College in 1896. Eight years later responsibility for its management passed to Huddersfield Borough Council.

By the First World War the College was educating over 1,800 students on a range of courses from day release apprentice training to higher education. The war stimulated growth at the College, largely due to the increased demand on the chemical and dye industries.

Similarly, the Second World war saw an increase in numbers, including trainee teachers evacuated from London, civilians, and forces personnel.

In the early 1950s the Ministry of Education proposed that a 'Branch College' be set up in the town for 'lower-level work' .The Local Education Authority (LEA) resolved to find accommodation for the Branch College. During this period the Technical College became known as Huddersfield College of Technology and the LEA included accommodation for the proposed Branch College in its plans for the Queensgate site now occupied by the University.

The Branch College was set up in 1963, using shared accommodation with the College of Technology and with a staff largely transferred from the 'tech'.

Huddersfield College of Education was established at Lindley and the secondary school at Salendine Nook was known as Huddersfield New College. The Local Education Authority now decided on the

Top left: *Craft workshop during the 1950s.* ***Left:*** *Early gym class.* ***Above:*** *Flower arranging.*

distinctive title of 'Ramsden Technical College' as a result of the Ramsden family's historic association with the town. Unfortunately, this led to enquiries as to the location of the town of Ramsden in Yorkshire!

Throughout the 1960s the Huddersfield College of Technology and the Ramsden Technical College shared resources, accommodation, equipment and staff.

Originally established with three departments, Engineering, General Studies and Science, the Ramsden Technical College was located in the 'Old Building', soon renamed 'The Ramsden Building', on Queensgate. This was far from adequate and the new College was forced to find extra accommodation where it could. During the academic year 1967-68, the Ramsden Technical College offered courses at over a dozen different locations.

In 1970 the Huddersfield College of Technology became a Polytechnic and the remaining lower level courses were taken over by the Ramsden Technical College. By the end of the decade the Ramsden Technical College was offering a wider range of courses in Mechanical and Electrical Engineering, Science, Business, Art & Design and GCSE '0' and 'A' Level subjects. A total of 4,165 students were enrolled for the first year of the College's existence in 1963, increasing to 7,549 by 1971.

The first Principal of the new Ramsden Technical College was appointed in 1965. Dr HT Taylor took this post with a brief to resolve the problems over accommodation. In 1965 the Royal Infirmary moved to Lindley leaving its New North Road site vacant. After a programme of refurbishment, Dr Taylor was able to move staff and students there in 1968. Following the recreation of the College of Technology into a Polytechnic in 1971 the Governors approved the name 'Huddersfield Technical College'.

The New North Road site enabled the College to consolidate most provision in one place and had sufficient land for additional building. This took place over the next 15 years, providing new accommodation for engineering, science, construction, and student services. Despite this, the College continued to use other buildings away from the New North Road campus.

In 1973, local secondary schools were reorganised creating three sixth form colleges in the town. Although competing for students in certain programme areas, there has been significant co-operation between Huddersfield New College, Greenhead College and Huddersfield Technical College. The College expanded the range of its provision of GCE '0' Levels (GCSEs) and 'A' Levels available to school leavers and adults.

During the late 1970s the unemployment rate in Huddersfield increased from 3.8 per rent in December 1978 to 12.6 per cent in January 1981. During this period many who, in better economic times, might have found employment after leaving school, stayed on in full time education. And many of those who were out of work attended classes to improve their employment prospects.

Top left: *Car maintenance in the 1970s.* ***Below:*** *Construction of the facilities at the New North Road site.*

DHSS regulations allowed unemployed people to enrol and the College was permitted to waive their course fees.

The College also expended considerable efforts in establishing training programmes to meet the requirements of various initiatives, such as the Youth Training Scheme.

In 1990 the College appointed Dr Malcolm Rossiter as Principal. Dr Rossiter was instrumental in guiding Huddersfield Technical College through the difficult period of incorporation, overseeing the transfer from the local authority to become an educational charitable trust. The College had to engage staff to manage finance and payroll, buildings, health and safety, caretaking and cleaning and many other functions.

The provision of Adult Education was transferred from LEA control to the College in 1993. The College now managed an extensive provision of courses delivered at community venues throughout the Huddersfield area. These courses ranged from academic programmes like GCSEs and 'A' levels to recreational courses like arts and crafts or sport.

In 1997 a new Principal was appointed. Ms Jeanne Coburn took over responsibility for the College in a period when financial constraints forced the College to restructure its staff, at the same time as meeting increasing; recruitment, retention and quality standards. The other key priority was to encourage the participation in further education by individuals and groups who had not previously benefited from the experience. The 'Widening Participation' agenda formed part of the Government's social inclusiveness policy designed to raise general standards of education throughout the UK.

Today, Kirklees College is one of the largest in the region, attracting students locally, nationally and internationally.

With 1,200 staff and over 23,000 students the College is a large community in its own right and its staff and students live in, work in and contribute to all the local communities that surround the College.

Meanwhile, investment continues. Work began on the Manchester Road site in November 2009. The multi-million pound building will replace the centre at New North Road. Covering 24,000 square metres, the development will be nine storeys high.

Kirklees College has also revealed plans for a new £7.5m engineering centre in Huddersfield. Not only will the innovative facility provide an exceptional learning environment for students on completion, but it will also provide current students with the

Top left: *Early computer classes.* ***Top right:*** *The College pictured in 2000.* ***Left and above:*** *Examples of full-time courses available at Kirklees College. The college's Travel and Tourism Course (left) offers opportunities starting from introductory courses right through to National Diploma level whilst their Animal Care course boasts some of the best facilities in the region. Their award-winning dedicated Taylor Hill Centre is an ideal venue.*

The finished design of the engineering facility will have many educational features such as technology display rooms showcasing renewable energy monitor boards and metal facade cladding to the exterior walls.

opportunity to engage in the design and build process of a live construction project.

The new building is due to open in September 2012 at the same time as the new centre at the Waterfront Quarter opens its doors on Manchester Road. The facilities will offer a state-of-the-art learning environment for future engineers and motor vehicle experts.

GMI Construction is due to undertake the design and build contracts for the new 5,500mÇ learning facility which will be built off St Andrew's Road in the town.

This project is the second phase of the proposal which was granted funding in September 2009 by the Learning and Skills Council. The addition of the college's engineering block will complement the modern architectural design to the campus, cementing Kirklees College's position as one of the leading colleges in the country.

With huge investment as well as the commitment to delivering courses through new technologies, Kirklees College will continue to develop and extend the range of learning and training it offers to the people of Huddersfield far into the 21st century.

Top left: *With an apprenticeship students get it all. They can train on the job, get qualified, get paid and get a career - all in one go.* ***Above left:*** *Childcare at Kirklees College. All of the 64 students studying on the level 2 Certificate in Childcare and Education at Kirklees College in 2011 passed their external examination in Safe, Healthy and Nurturing Environments for Children.* ***Below:*** *An artist's impression of the new Waterfront Quarter entrance.*

Richard Carter Ltd

The Original Hand Tool Manufacturer

Not sure if it's a spade or a shovel? Honley-based Richard Carter Ltd can certainly answer that question for you.

Few British companies can trace their traditions as far back as Richard Carter Ltd, the original hand tool manufacturer. With getting on for 300 years of experience, the name of Richard Carter Ltd has become synonymous with shovels – not least the world-famous 'Carter Shovel' available today in a variety of styles and sizes, finished with handles which complement the tool, made from wood, metal, fibreglass or polyfibre.

The earliest records mention one David Carter, who in 1695 was carrying on a business as a blacksmith in Deighton.

David Carter had three sons. The youngest, born in 1728, was named Jeremiah.

Jeremiah Carter moved the blacksmith business to Highburton in 1740.

In 1850 Jeremiah's great, great grandson, Richard Carter, relocated the firm to Dene Works in Kirkburton, which was to be its home for the next 150 years. Richard Carter now formed a partnership with a distant cousin, Ben Carter, the pair trading under the name of B & R Carter Blacksmiths and Edge Tool makers. By the mid-1850s the firm had become well known as manufacturers of high quality cloggers, knives, hay cutting spades and chipping knives.

Richard Carter introduced steam for power to the firm, and gas for lighting; woodworking machinery too was installed and he began importing hickory timber from the USA.

In the 1870s Richard Carter and his son Robert were by now describing themselves as 'Shovel makers', meeting the ever-increasing demand for shovels from the rapidly expanding coal mining industries of Yorkshire and Nottinghamshire.

By the end of the 19th century the firm had installed copying lathes, and was not only producing tool handles for its own products but was also making large quantities of handles for other tool makers.

Top: *A 19th century image of the Carters in Highburton.* ***Left:*** *Stanley Carter shaping shovels.*

The next generation of the family had joined the firm by the start of the 20th century: Stanley Carter and his brothers Eric, Francis and Ernest. Ernest served in World War I but was tragically killed in Gallipoli in 1917, having returned to his unit on the same day as his wedding. He was 26 years old.

Richard Carter Ltd was incorporated in 1909. Five years later the First World War broke out and demand for the company's tools increased dramatically. Every week, thousands of shovels were sent via Kirkburton village railway station to the troops on the front line. And history would repeat itself when the Second World War placed even greater demands on the company's services.

Having survived unscathed through two world wars the future for the firm was potentially a rosy one. Yet having avoided the attentions of the Luftwaffe the post war years would witness a disaster for the company, no less destructive than if it had been bombed.

By now, following the retirement of Stanley Carter in the 1940s, (who only stopped working following a stroke whilst in his late seventies), his sons Duncan and Philip were running the company.

The firm had always been cautious and careful to guard against any risk of fire, particularly with so much dry timber shavings about.

Smoking was not allowed. All electrics were made dead at finishing time by opening the circuit-breaker in the sub-station.

Wood shavings had to be taken outside and burnt. Later a fan and ducting system was installed to blow them from the machine into a brick-built outhouse.

On 26 January, 1957, a large pile was set alight. Seemingly it burnt out well before closing time, but left a few red embers. The wind increased during the night and sparks were blown under the eaves. Fire rapidly took hold of the dust that had attached itself underneath the wooden roof.

The first warning was given by one of the firm's tenants, Mr D Barraclough, who lived at 52, North Road. He was a light sleeper; he got up to investigate and phoned the Fire Brigade. Shortly afterwards Duncan Carter saw it from his home in Hallas Road. Phillip Carter received a phone call at 3.15 a.m. and was at the works by 3.30.

The whole of the wood-working shed, 120 ft long,

Top left: *Eric Carter putting the finishing touches to a handle in 1933.* ***Below:*** *Duncan Carter on the lathe.* ***Above:*** *Tools of the trade.*

was ablaze from end to end, flames shooting up to 60 ft. high.

Four brigades attended and tapped the local hydrants, but they required much more water. A pump drew water from the dam at Springfield Mill and a pipe conveyed it the length of the village.

A further pump was placed in the stream at Riley Bottom and there was a tangle of hose pipes everywhere. The police closed the road at 3.30 a.m. diverting all traffic by way of Penistone Road and Shelley until 7 a.m. It was the biggest fire within living memory in Kirkburton.

With daylight the scene was one of devastation. The outer walls still stood but the roof beams were reduced to only a quarter of their cross-section. All the machines had suffered badly. Piles of hickory were now just charcoal.

By 8 a.m. everybody began the task of clearing up - shovelling through tons of rubble and salvaging anything useful.

There was a serious financial loss, because although insurance fully covered the stock and machinery, the building was very much under-insured. A helpful fire assessor, however, enabled a better than expected settlement to be obtained.

Many of the machines were re-built by Gill's, the first being the tapering machine. Although they had good stocks of shovel shafts undamaged by the fire, they had to buy large quantities of 28" straight blunt from Arthur Burroughs & Co. Ltd., of Liverpool, to taper these as required.

It was essential to keep customers going and turnover up: all the work of sanding shafts, packing up and completion of orders had to be done in the shovel shop. Staff worked every evening until 9 p.m. and all through Saturdays for many weeks until the premises were rebuilt and things returned to normal.

Meanwhile the disposal of shavings remained a problem.

An electric baling press was obtained. Bales weighing nearly three quarters of a hundredweight were made and stacked up outside. Several loads of these were sold for what they cost to produce, and many more given away. Some shavings were taken to mills to burn in their boiler fires. Eventually Carters found local farmers who could use the waste material for bedding.

The 1970s saw the beginning of the decline of the nationalised coal and steel industries and this forced the company to seek new markets. This was so successful that, despite many alterations to the Kirkburton premises during the 1980s, the company outgrew Dene Works and began the search for a new home.

As around the same time was today's Managing Director Richard Carter when a surprising coincidence occurred. Prior to getting married in 1985, Richard and his wife to be, Charmaine, were looking for a house in the Kirkburton/Highburton area. Whilst Charmaine was working one Sunday Richard saw a house that he thought was 'the one' without even viewing it. They arranged a hasty viewing and found that the house was built by a J & E Carter in the early 1800s...they bought the house.

One day whilst viewing his late father's postcard collection Richard noticed a photo/postcard which was

Left and above: *At work in 1978.*

taken part way up Far Dene in Highburton. This showed a large chimney towering above the house, the remains of which were now in his garden. It turned out that the garden was originally the 'Engine Shed' for the building next door, the original home/forge for the Company!

Later the couple were fortunate enough to buy a piece of connected land to extend their garden. Whilst rebuilding a number of old walls, Richard recovered several old grind wheels/stones that are believed to have been used in the original forge to sharpen agricultural tools and knives...he still has them today.

Eventually, in 1999, the firm moved to its current home, the historic Neiley Works in Brockholes. The new premises provided the opportunity to embrace state-of-the-art manufacturing techniques which, combined with the company's heritage, enabled it to simultaneously improve design and enhance quality.

Back in the early 1800s the Neiley Works had been used as a tannery. From the 1830s onwards candles were made there, and from the 1960s it had been the manufacturing site for 'Kiwi' boot polish and moth balls.

Alterations to the site took two years. Carters moved in May 1999, having built two new sheds, completely rewired and modernised the premises, and having also demolished the old mill-owners' house to make way for a car park.

The fire precautions were uprated. Ironically then, in July 2002, the factory was on the receiving end of a flash flood that caused over £100,000 of damage. The depth of water on the roller shutter doors was such that they buckled under the weight. Clearing the mess took several weeks, but with the help of the workforce limited production was up and running in a few days.

Richard Carter and Philip Everitt had been running the company as Joint MDs since the retirement of Richard's father Duncan in 1990.

Philip Everitt retired in 2010. The ownership of the company is now fully back with the Carter family, led by Richard Carter.

Today, beyond it's general range of products which can be viewed on the company's website, www.richardcarterltd.co.uk, the company also does contract woodturning for such products as coffin handles and chimney sweep brooms. Exports go as far afield as Dubai, Spain, Ireland, the West Indies and Germany.

Nearly three centuries since the firm's founder, Jeremiah Carter, started his own business the Carter family is proud of the fact that they still own and run Richard Carter Ltd. But they are prouder still of the people who work for the company, many of whom have done so for many years. Some may see tradition and innovation as unlikely bedfellows, but for Richard Carter Ltd they define exactly what the company stands for.

Above: *The photograph found by Richard Carter of Far Dene, Highburton, showing the chimney of the old Carter spade factory.* ***Left and below:*** *Recent views inside the factory.*

J & E Dickinson - Longley Farm

Rising to the Top

Today Longley Farm is best known for its dairy products such as fresh cream, yogurt and cottage cheese. But these are relatively recent achievements. The family connection with Longley certainly goes back to the late seventeenth century through the Dickinsons and then, originally, the Hinchliffes. In those very early days the main activity was textiles based on hand-woven wool cloth. This trade flourished until the coming of the mills and after at least 250 years in hand weaving, by 1860 Longley was no longer active in the textile trade.

The shift from weaving to farming as the main business was massive and running a small hill farm in the Pennine Uplands was not easy. So, by the time that brothers Joseph and Edgar Dickinson inherited the farm in 1948, it was in a poor state. Upper Longley Farm was bequeathed to them by their great uncle, Jonas Hinchliffe. With it came 40 acres, ten cows, a Clydesdale horse and debts greater than the value of the legacy!

A year later the brothers were able to buy the 30 acre Lower Longley Farm at auction for £2,350. The circumstances here were similar. Another branch of the Hinchliffe family had shifted from weaving to farming, but had also diversified by running a small shop. This shop did well, serving the very large community, especially those working in the local quarries: famed for stone flags. But the quarries went and so did the shop.

The Dickinson brothers came from a farming and dairying background. Their father Edgar Dickinson senior had been a farm contractor based at Field Head Farm, in Shepley, and had also run a dairy business, the Abbey Dairy, in the 1920s and 1930s. The brothers were brought up in a stimulating business environment which combined farming, engineering and milk processing.

Rambler, the steam traction engine, was brought out of retirement during the Second World War by Edgar Dickinson snr and was well known in the area moving from farm to farm with its threshing machine. Meanwhile, the brothers both became apprentice engineers. At the start of the war, Edgar remained at Hopkinson's, whilst Joseph left Broadbent's in 1940 to join the Royal Navy.

In 1944, Edgar joined his father in contracting to keep up with the need to thresh the corn that had been introduced as part of the emergency measures brought in by the Ministry of Food. After demobilisation in 1946, Joseph, despite being an experienced engineering officer, faced a difficult time as the post-war economy ran down. However, in 1948 they had the chance to get back into farming. At the outset, Edgar kept up the contracting business whilst Joseph took care of the farm.

At first they kept sheep and poultry, and grew turnips and potatoes, as well as bottling milk. Highly progressive, their milk was not only free from tuberculosis but also pasteurised.

Top: *Longley Farm.* ***Left:*** *Edgar Dickinson Snr delivering TT milk around Shepley at 4d a pint.* ***Above:*** *Joseph and Edgar Dickinson pictured in 1960 loading bottles of cream for delivery.*

By 1953 the brothers had moved from hand-milking in a barn to machine-milking in a milking parlour. Milk was sold to Barnsley and Huddersfield Co-ops. They also bought a separator and began making cream; the first major outlet being a stall on Oldham Market. The growth of this new business saw Edgar give up contracting and move full-time into milk processing.

A licence was obtained from the Milk Marketing Board in 1954 to take in milk from other farms for processing. The brothers now began to build up a modest daily intake of 200 gallons, selling the produce over a 30-mile wide area.

By the 1960s Longley Farm had become one of the largest private creameries in the country, producing up to 40,000 gallons of cream each month. Investment continued, and in 1969, a dam was built for cooling water and back up electrical generators were installed to insure against any future power failures. That same year the firm began producing its award-winning yoghurt.

In 1972 cottage cheese was being made: the first time it had been made on a large scale anywhere outside the USA.

Tyers Hall Farm, in Barnsley, was acquired in 1973 and still specialises in producing high quality Jersey milk.

The milk used in Longley Farm's products is supplied by its own herd of Jersey cows and those belonging to 24 dedicated Jersey farmers around the region. In addition, a second group of 17 local farmers provide a lower butterfat milk, mainly from Friesians, which is ideal for making products such as whipping cream.

Longley Farm processes about 40 million litres of milk a year, which goes into its curd, butter, cottage cheese, soft cheese, yoghurt and cream products. Much of the original farm remains, but it now nestles amongst a highly efficient, ultra modern business, belying its rustic exterior.

By the early 1990s, with frozen cream, Longley Farm had become Britain's largest exporter of frozen food outside the EEC. Development would continue in the late 1990s with the establishment of dairies in Estonia and Australia and most recently an operation in Uruguay.

The brothers, Joseph OBE and Edgar MBE, retired in 1997 and the business is now run by Joseph's son, Jimmy. There is a strong sense of history and tradition at Longley Farm; and if there is one thing that history teaches, it is that change is inevitable. But, although technology may change, the human spirit and the desire to succeed endure.

There's never a dull moment at Longley Farm.

Top left: *Vera Jessop filling cream by jug and hand capping the foil lids. Paper cartons were being tried as replacements for glass bottles.* ***Above:*** *May 1954 in the yard at Upper Longley Farm, with grey Ferguson tractor - from left Kenneth Heeley, Maurice Major, Dennis Charlesworth, Edgar Dickinson and Joseph Dickinson. Maurice Major worked at Longley Farm for 45 years from 1951 until he retired in 1996.* ***Centre:*** *A selection of Longley Farm products.* ***Below:*** *Longley Farm livery.*

Pearson Funeral Service - The Family Firm Who Care

Death and taxes are said to be the only certainties in life. A little fiscal ingenuity may help avoid taxes, but none of us avoid the passage of time and its inevitable consequence. In the distant past funerals for the wealthy may have been elaborate affairs, but for poorer folk there was likely to be a laying out by a local women who was also the local midwife, followed by resting at peace in an open coffin made by a local carpenter, on display at home until the day of the actual burial service.

Today, by contrast, everyone benefits from the services of professional undertakers who remove much of the organisational burden from the shoulders of bereaved families, whether they be rich or poor.

One of the most highly respected firms in the Huddersfield area is the Pearson Funeral Service, based in Manchester Road, Marsden. Serving both Huddersfield and Saddleworth, the firm traces its origins back to the early decades of the 20th century. It was in 1920 that 23-year-old Alfred Bagley established a joinery business and funeral service based in the now demolished Old Silk Mill at Warehouse Hill.

Alfred was the son of the Station Master at Marsden. After having trained as a master joiner he had originally set up a joiners shop in a converted blacksmith's premises on Manchester Road. Alfred's wife, Carrie, did the clerical work, looking after the telephone and office.

The Bagleys' son, Peter later joined the family firm, eventually taking over the business from his father in 1962. Founder, Alfred Bagley, died in 1982 at the age of 84.

The firm was taken over by Clive Pearson in 2003 when Peter Bagley took semi-retirement. Clive Pearson trained locally as a funeral director and embalmer from the age of 15. Clive has other skills too: he recalls arriving at a church for a

***Top left:** Founder, Alfred Bagely. **Above:** Peter Bagley pictured in 2005. **Below** Pearson Funeral Service's premises, 2005.*

funeral only to discover that the organist was being driven away in the back of an ambulance. Luckily Clive plays the organ and was able to step into the breach. Nothing is too much trouble.

Clive also recalls an occasion when he and his drivers had to act as waiters and barmen when a hotel booked to provide a funeral tea had forgotten to put the event in their diary.

Today, at Pearsons Funeral Service all coffins are bought-in which results in a far larger choice than in the past. Not much else had changed down the years: until 1957, when the chapel of rest opened, the deceased were laid out at home; and hearses and limousines were hired from carriage masters rather than being owned by the firm. Now Pearson's owns its own immaculately presented Mercedes hearse and limousines.

Until the 1930s, when a crematorium opened in Leeds, there was no alternative to burial - the Huddersfield crematorium opened in 1957. Costs, too, have changed significantly: in the 1930s a burial cost as little as £21 while today up to £4,000 is not unusual.

The funeral home in Marsden was fully renovated in 2005. A chapel of rest opened in Meltham in 2006, and another in Holmfirth in 2007.

Meanwhile, funerals are getting more eco-friendly with some 'green' funerals taking place in woodland settings: a broader range of coffins is now used with wicker, bamboo, cardboard and even picture coffins on offer.

Yet though much has changed, some things remain unaltered: this family business still provides a careful, caring service, sensitive to its clients' needs, 24 hours each day on 365 days a year.

Clive Pearson took the position of Chairman of the British Institute of Funeral Directors for Yorkshire in 2009. In 2013 he will take the postion of Chairman of the British Institute of Embalmers for Yorkshire as well as President of the National Association of Funeral Directors for the county.

But it's not been all business for Clive; in 2007 he married Leanne who, most appropriatly he had met at a funeral tea. Leanne too is now working in the business – and with three daughters - Rebecca, Abbieleigh and Bethany - the family baton may one day be passed to a new generation.

Meanwhile, the Pearson family's professional reputation has been built on trust and recommendation; they have become known as the family firm who care.

Above: *Clive Pearson pictured alongside the firm's Mercedes hearse and limousine.* ***Below:*** *Clive pictured outside Pearson Funeral Service's Marsden premises.*

Crowther & Shaw - A Cool Company

From pre-war domestic and commercial refrigerators to today's sophisticated cold stores, air conditioning, cooling and ventilation systems Crowther & Shaw Limited have always been prepared to move with the times.

Crowther & Shaw Limited, now located in Queens Mill Road, Huddersfield, started as a family business in the 1920s based in premises in Market Street. Established as plumbers and electrical engineers, it was during the 1930s, through installing cold rooms for local butchers and meat wholesalers, that the business began its move into its current marketplace.

Following the Second World War Crowther & Shaw began to concentrate on the expanding commercial refrigeration sector, a market the company remains active in to this day.

During the 1980s the company also incorporated air conditioning into its portfolio, a sector which over the following decades would become the growth market within the refrigeration industry.

"We have grown from a local supplier to one with a national identity serving clients throughout the UK from our Huddersfield base," says Managing Director, Mark Gledhill.

Following the demise of Messrs Crowther and Shaw the company was owned by three generations of the Douglas family until 2006 when the business was sold to Martin Howlett and Mark Gledhill. Both Mark and Martin had served their apprenticeships at Crowther & Shaw, Mark from the mid-80's and Martin the mid-90's. According to Mark: "We hope to continue and add to the proud history of one of Huddersfield's famous businesses and while we value the links with our past, we are conscious of utilising modern technology to the benefit of our clients in the future."

In the past 20 years the company has expanded the business to take in projects all around the UK. Services on offer include the design and installation of air conditioning, ventilation and refrigeration systems along with 24 hour, 365 day service and maintenance support.

The company currently serves over 1,500 sites throughout the UK for a wide range of clients, from local independent clients to large multi-national operations.

Mark says: "While our larger clients place more demands on our time we are extremely pleased that many of our customers have been with us for many years, some for over 30. It is satisfying to know that we have grown alongside many such businesses and have been able to provide them with the required level of service for so long. Many of our customers sign up to maintenance contracts with us which provide them with the comfort of regular planned maintenance to reduce plant failures and the knowledge that if something should fail they can call us 24 hours a day 365 days a year and we will be there for them."

Top left: *Arthur Douglas pictured alongside one of the first Kelvinator refrigerators.* ***Above:*** *Geoffrey Douglas advertising Crowther & Shaw at a trade fair during the 1960s.* ***Left:*** *The Crowther & Shaw fleet in the early 1980s.*

The company has over 400 such contracts including Local Authorities such as Kirklees, Wakefield and Barnsley, NHS Trusts such as Calderdale & Kirklees, Hull and Leeds, as well as well known high street names such as Royal Bank of Scotland, McDonalds, Holiday Inn and the universities in Huddersfield and Manchester.

Crowther & Shaw now operates a state-of-the-art computer system to monitor its service operation. This allows 'real time' access to its engineers via 'Personal Digital Assistants' resulting in faster repair times, component ordering and service response.

Today, the company employs some 20 engineers based in Yorkshire, Lancashire, Humberside and the Midlands. All are fully qualified with either City & Guilds or NVQ qualifications including the new refrigerant handling qualifications.

Part of Crowther & Shaw's success has been down to developing its own staff.

"Over the past 15 years we have employed up to three apprentices most summers with a view to growing our own engineers," says Mark. "While it is always difficult to judge a school leaver's potential we have had an excellent success rate in creating capable and well-qualified engineers for our industry."

The company has had many apprentice winners of the Yorkshire and Humberside regional training award from the HVCA, along with two winners of the prestigious national Refrigeration and Air Conditioning (RAC) Student of the Year Award, firstly Martin Howlett in 1996 followed by Tom Betts in 2005.

Tom Howard won the 2006 HVCA award while Matthew Lander won the UK Skillfridge Competition and a place representing the United Kingdom at the World Skills in Japan at the end of 2007 - a practical rather than college-based challenge described as "The Olympics" for tradespeople.

While proud of their younger generation, Crowther & Shaw are also proud of a long serving member of staff. "While I have been at the company for 25 years", says Mark, "Robert Turner, our senior service engineer, has just completed 32 years service, something which in this day and age is almost unknown. Hopefully some of our younger engineers can also follow that path!"

Top: *Part of Crowther & Shaw's 2011 team.* ***Left:*** *Crowther & Shaw company management and senior staff led by Andrew Douglas, circa 1995.* ***Above right:*** *Efficient air conditioning systems improve people's working environments.* ***Below:*** *Managing Director Mark Gledhill and senior engineer Robert Turner celebrate his 30 years' service in 2008.*

Taylor & Lodge - Cloth Fit For a King

For the James Bond film 'Quantum Of Solace' Daniel Craig wore an iconic black dinner jacket. Its fabric was woven exclusively by Taylor & Lodge at its factory In Huddersfield for the American designer Tom Ford. Taylor & Lodge customer Tom Ford was hired to design Bond's suits to give them an edgier feel and look, like those of Sean Connery's classic Bond of the 1960s.

Weaving has been going on in the Huddersfield area for centuries. Records indicate that there was a Roger the Fuller (Fulling is a process where the woollen material was pounded in water to make it thicken) living at Holme in 1274.

Since the 1960s many of Huddersfield's weaving mills have closed down, victims of recession and foreign competition. But there always remains room at the top: the best have survived.

Taylor & Lodge, incorporated as Rashcliffe Mills Ltd, was founded in 1883. It has occupied Rashcliffe Mills, at Albert Street, in Lockwood, ever since. The company still carries out all aspects of fine worsted cloth production, combining traditional methods and skills with the best of modern technology.

In the warp preparation room a fully automatic 'Uster' drawing machine is used, the first of its kind to be operated in the UK textile industry. High speed 'Dornier' rapier looms in the weaving department ensure the precision and accuracy which is essential in the production of fine micron wool cloths, using superfine worsted yarn counts.

Fabric weights produced range from 165 grammes per square metre to 700 gms. Computerised pattern weaving looms make the sample production unit one of the most modern in the country. A large selection of suiting, jacketing and dishdasha cloths is created each season. What is a dishdasha? The word serves to underline the truly international scope of Taylor & Lodge's business - a dishdasha is the long robe with sleeves frequently worn by men in Arabia and beyond.

Above: *An example of the finest quality of Superfine Worsted suits made by Taylor & Lodge.* ***Below:*** *Rashcliffe Mills, the home of Taylor & Lodge for over one hundred years.*

A selection of cloths is shown at international exhibitions such as Premiere Vision in Paris, and during shows in London, Tokyo, Seoul, Hong Kong, Shanghai and New York. More than 80 per cent of production is exported, the main markets being Japan, the Far and Middle East and Europe.

Only natural fibres are used in production, usually superfine wool, cashmere, silk and summer kid mohair, but also rare fibres such as mink, sable, ermine and vicuna. The company is a founder member of the Lumb's Huddersfield Golden Bale Club and is still very proud to be a user of those hand-sorted wools. The company is also a member of the British Escorial Wool Guild and the Australian Superfine Wool Growers' Association. In 1966 the company won the Queen's Award for Exporting, becoming the very first textile concern to receive one. Today Taylor & Lodge is deservedly recognised as the manufacturer of the finest and most luxurious cloths in the world. The company was acquired by the Bradford-based Bulmer and Lumb Group in 2005, helping ensure the long term future of the workforce.

In November 2010, the company was honoured by a personal visit from the Prince of Wales. Taylor & Lodge is very proud to be associated with The Prince of Wales Wool Campaign, of which Prince Charles is Patron, promoting the importance of wool as a natural and sustainable fibre.

For Prince William's marriage to Kate Middleton on 29 April, 2011, Taylor & Lodge commissioned a special woven suit length for him. The cloth was designed, woven and finished at Taylor & Lodge. The yarn for this cloth was sourced by the AWI (Australian Wool Innovation) and the wool growers of Australia in a specially produced blend of wool which was then spun into yarn by Bulmer and Lumb.

Taylor & Lodge launched a new web site and online store in 2011. It offers the opportunity to purchase suit lengths directly from the factory. Suits lengths can even but purchased in a gift box complete with a certificate of authenticity stating that the cloth is designed, woven and finished in Huddersfield. A true 'Made in England' product.

From James Bond to Royalty, the firm of Taylor & Lodge ensures that Huddersfield retains its reputation as the home of the world's finest worsted cloth.

Top and above left: *Taylor & Lodge's weaving department in 2005.* ***Above left:*** *The actual cloth for HRH Prince William's marriage in April 2011. Note the Woolmark Gold trademark symbolising the highest quality.* ***Below:*** *At work inside Taylor & Lodge in 2011.*

Holmfirth Dyers Ltd - Chasing the Rainbow

The practice of dyeing cloth is almost as old as weaving. However, dyeing very soon became a trade separate to that of weaving. Both an art and a science, dyeing is a far trickier business than one might imagine; an awful lot of knowledge and skill goes into ensuring that customers get the exact shade of colour they specify, time after time.

Holmfirth Dyers Ltd is based at Ribbleden Dye Works, Holmfirth. At the firm's premises in Dunford Road, commission dyeing and finishing processes are carried out for customers throughout the United Kingdom and abroad.

The business was founded in 1985 by Brian Duckett. Brian had previously been the dye house manager at Whiteley and Green Ltd, another well-known local business.

Though Holmfirth Dyers has today some 60 staff, back in 1985 there were only 11 employees, including Brian's wife Pearl, and later on their son Martin joined the company.

Pearl ran the office whilst Brian, advised by Charles Whitely, concentrated on the business of dyeing. When Martin joined the family business he too at first concentrated on dyeing, being taught the trade by an old hand, Herbert Shaw, before moving into production alongside Brian. As well as running the office, Pearl also drove the wagons in those early days.

Setting out as loose stock and wet piece dyers, the early years were dominated by a struggle to deal with the problems associated with unsafe buildings and outdated machinery.

All these problems have been efficiently dealt with over the years through continuing re-investment by the company in plant, machinery and buildings

In 2004 the company upgraded to the latest version of Bespoke Textile Computer Systems Textile Management System. The new

Top: *An elevated view of Holmfirth Dyers.* ***Left:*** *Two of the company's vehicles in the 1990s.* ***Above:*** *Sample dyeing on a Pattern machine*

system manages the receipt of the 'greige' pieces (un-dyed cloth), allocation of those pieces to orders, receipt of finished pieces from work, dispatch and invoicing, and features a more intuitive and graphical interface than the previous version. After having used the previous Bespoke system for 14 years, Holmfirth Dyers decided to upgrade to the new system in order to improve work flow and increase ease of operator use. Geoff Goodman, financial controller and project manager, was delighted with the speed and efficiency of the installation, which was carried out with the minimum of disruption.

Today, the firm's main markets are the armed forces, upholstery and fine worsteds, supplying large textile enterprises such as Camira Fabrics and the Bulmer & Lumb Group.

Originally the firm dyed only wool pieces; today not only wool but also polyester and cotton have been added to the fabrics which are dyed to the highest standards using high temperature dyeing vessels, low-liquid drying and the most modern machinery.

Delivering on time and giving customers what they want has been the key to progress within the company, and a belief that nothing is impossible has been the company's watchword from the outset.

Meanwhile, for Holmfirth Dyers, community involvement is as important as the work done in the dye works. Many companies are besieged with requests from charities and it is hard to refuse anyone. However, it was decided that Kirkwood Hospice would be the main charity that the firm would support as it provided a worthwhile service for local people.

Over the years the company's representatives have attended events and sponsored various activities in support of the Hospice.

From the year 2000 the firm undertook sponsoring the 'Annual Dinner'. This was an event that provided fundraising, along with a chance for all Kirkwood supporters to get together and enjoy themselves. These events have raised many thousands of pounds and Holmfirth Dyers is proud to be associated with Kirkwood Hospice and hopes to continue its association for many years to come.

Above left: *Drying fabric on the Tenter.* ***Above:*** *Processing fabric through the cropping machine.* ***Below:*** *Loading a Jet dyeing machine*

Longley Park Motors - 30 Great Years

Based at the Triangle, Paddock, Longley Park Motors Ltd, trading as Longley Park Kia, is one of Huddersfield's best known car dealers.

The firm celebrated its 30th birthday in 2011. It was on 1 March, 1981, that Longley Park Motors first opened for trading.

It was certainly an interesting year. The highlight was the wedding of Prince Charles to Lady Diana Spencer.

In the motoring world petrol stations start selling motor fuel by the litre –disguising the fact that inflation was running at an annual rate of 11 per cent.

British Leyland launched the Triumph Acclaim. Within months, however, BL announced the closure of three factories - a move which would cost nearly 3,000 jobs. Unemployment passed the 2,500,000 mark for the first time in nearly 50 years.

Longley Park Motors was founded by local garage boss Tony Baines. Despite the grim economic outlook he took a gamble to set up his own dealership. He called it Longley Park Motors – since at that time the firm was based near Longley Park. The firm would eventually relocate to its present premises in Paddock in 1989.

Tony, an accomplished rally driver in the 60s and 70s had previously become a well respected manager in the local motor industry through his honesty, decisive nature and hard work. After opening, excellent sales of Lada cars in Huddersfield was the making of his business.

The firm would continue to be a Lada dealership from 1981 until 1995. By then the firm had already been a dealer for Proton since 1989, an arrangement which would continue until 1998. Two years earlier the firm had begun selling Skoda cars.

Longley Park Motors would continue as Skoda dealers until 2003. The present day Kia dealership began in 2002.

The business is unique; it has survived in a ruthless and competitive sector with the philosophy of offering all customers and visitors a satisfying and comfortable experience. Longley

***Top:** Where it all began - Longley Park Motors' first premises at the bottom of Somerset Road in 1981. **Centre:** A flying Lada driven by Tony Baines, navigated by John Waite during the 1980s Lada Challenge Events. **Left and above:** Longley Park Motors under their former Lada (left) and Proton (above) dealerships.*

Park is somewhere different, where each customer's values and expectations are attempted to be matched, rather than one-size fits all. The range of products has changed and developed beyond recognition over 30 years, but the service and the value for money offer has remained the same throughout. The company offers some unique services such as a free loan car to all its clients. This keeps them mobile when off the road for service or unexpected repairs.

A genuine friendly and trustworthy approach has always been the Longley Park way of doing things; customers are part of the team, all of this in a relaxed environment.

The company and directors have never been greedy, even in the good times, and have always tried to do the right thing by customers and staff, always ethical, always thinking and acting long term. This, it could be argued, could hold the company back from serious growth, but the health and wellbeing of the customers, staff and the business has always remained the driving force.

In 2003 Longley Park KIA Motors were proud to be the main sponsor for the Huddersfield Giants.

The company has witnessed the failure of many similar businesses during the last three decades and it does not intend to become one of them. The business expanded and invested heavily in 2008, opening a brand new after-sales facility incorporating all the very latest technology, equipment and customer comforts. It created easy parking for customers and a much better working environment for staff. This in turn has made more room for the development of a larger sales area.

In 2009 and 2010 all previous sales records were broken. KIA Motors brought that massive sales growth, and gave customers old and new, much satisfaction. KIA is clearly a winner, with a unique seven year warranty, the very latest technology with designs, and styles that customers want to be seen in.

Longley Park Motors employs a diligent, skilled workforce of 16 local people. The company has a turnover of over £6 million, and is a positive, contributing force to the local economy. It is a genuine business which clients can trust, out to satisfy all local motoring needs.

Company founder Tony Baines died in 2008; but it is a continuing testimony to his character that Longley Park Motors is still a successful and unique dealership. The business is family run to the present day with the values espoused, and the reputation earned by Tony still fully intact.

Top left: *A busy 1984 showroom at a Lada open day.* ***Above left:*** *John Waite delivering 10 New Skoda models to the Huddersfield Giants in 1999 .* ***Above:*** *Managing Director John Waite (5th from right) and members of his team at Longley Park Motors, 2009.* ***Below:*** *Longley Park Motors pictured in 2009.*

H. Downs & Sons

Casting a Name for Quality

A two-tonne giant has become a familiar figure outside a Huddersfield foundry. The sculpture was created as a novel sign for the H Downs & Sons iron foundry in Leeds Road. It was cast by the foundry, following its commission by Alan and Nigel Downs, joint managing directors of the firm, which is based at the Peacock Works.

The foundry turns out 30 to 40 pieces of art each year, on top of the engineering castings that are its main business.

The company was started in 1946 by Walter Downs and his father Horace.

Following his release from HM Forces in 1945, after some time spent in hospital, Walter Downs got a job as an office clerk at a small iron foundry. Walter soon found out that the company was losing money.

Walter could see his job slipping away and made a reckless decision. During the months he had been in hospital he had received little of his Army pay and had saved £200 which he offered to lend his boss. The owner accepted Walter's offer and promised to make him a director.

Two days later a supplier rang saying a cheque had been returned marked 'Refer to Drawer.'

That weekend Walter's father Horace came home on demobilisation leave. He and Walter decided to visit the foundry owner at his home. The owner confessed that he had lost the whole £200 gambling. Horace and Walter agreed to put another £250 into the business on the condition that they, not the owner, controlled the cash flow.

Three weeks later it emerged that the owner had put the £250 into another bank account and business cheques were bouncing yet again.

With bills unpaid the business was put up for auction.

The assets were mainly fixtures in the building: the crane, furnace and grinding machines and it was not convenient to move them. Walter and his father bought everything for knockdown prices, using £500 borrowed from Horace's sister. They began work again on 1 April, 1946, as H. Downs & Sons (Huddersfield) Ltd.

All the equipment in the foundry was antiquated: the crane was manually operated by ropes and was very slow. The furnace consisted of a steel tube lined with firebricks and the metal requiring to be melted had to be hand cranked to a rickety old platform ten feet above the ground. Soon, however, the place was buzzing.

Top: *Horace (left) and Walter Downs.* ***Left:*** *Pattern-making at H. Downs & Sons.* ***Above:*** *The H. Down & Sons statue.*

Walter and Horace were able to accumulate some surplus money which was used to electrify the crane. They also invested in a second-hand Canadian Army lorry. The workforce now increased to twelve men, and output was trebled, enabling them to repay the £500 they had borrowed.

But the landlord had doubled the rent when Walter and Horace had taken over the lease. When Walter and Horace themselves paid to replace the roof the landlord said he would put up the rent again when the lease was due for renewal.

Happily, a helpful Factory Inspector told Walter about a site where a new foundry could be built.

Sadly, Horace passed away, receiving a full military funeral in recognition of his Army service.

Meanwhile building work went ahead. The old landlord found out about the new foundry only when Walter told him they would not be renewing the lease.

During the 1970s two of Walter's three sons, Alan and Nigel, entered the family business. In the 1980s more technological developments were required, whilst the limit to the maximum casting size was raised from 2 tons to 5 tons.

In 1986 H. Downs & Sons acquired John Booth's, of Ripponden. The two foundries together were capable of offering a significantly wider range of iron alloys.

1993 saw the arrival of computers and a bespoke system, designed by the brothers, for the control of pattern equipment, production control and accounts.

The late 1990s brought about investment in the environment, beginning with the purchase of a new cupola furnace in Huddersfield, closely followed by a sand knockout and reclamation unit for John Booth's. A similar unit was installed in Huddersfield in 1998.

2005 saw the transfer of personnel, equipment and business to Huddersfield and the amalgamation of John Booth's with H. Downs and Sons. This followed the acquisition of the adjacent St John's works site and resulted in a considerable expansion. Capacity was hugely increased and technological advances brought the introduction of new material types, most notably, ni-hard and ni-resist irons.

In 2011 the company was awarded with the ISO 9001, an affirmation of its up-to-date methods and stringent systems.

Today, H Downs & Sons Ltd enjoys a well deserved reputation for offering some of the most advanced foundry services, and for retaining all the entrepreneurial zeal first exhibited by its founders so many years ago.

Top left *The mixing of molten iron to produce special iron alloys.* ***Below:*** *A non-magnetic ductile iron casting. This stator end for a Canadian power station weighed 3800kgs. In the background is a 4200kg machine tool bed.*

Dugdale Bros. & Co - Cloth of Distinction

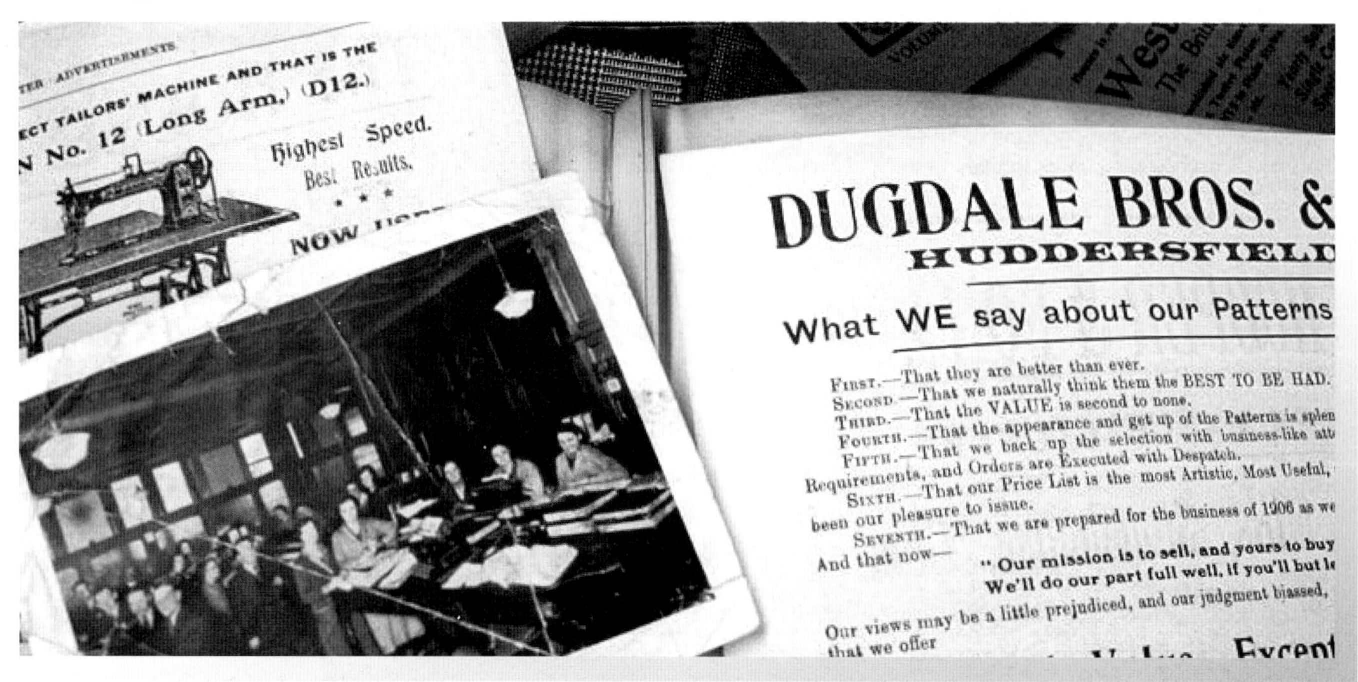

It was back in 1896 that two brothers, Henry Percy and Frederick Herbert Dugdale established their cloth merchants business in Huddersfield, the centre of Britain's fine worsted industry.

Using skilled designers, weavers and finishers the Dugdale brothers' range of cloths soon found favour with the finest tailors and their reputation quickly spread throughout Europe and the Americas. Today, based at 5 Northumberland Street, Dugdale Brothers and Company Limited, remains an exclusive designer fabric merchant and supplier to Savile Row, and to the finest tailors, couturiers and retailers throughout the world.

From the very outset in 1896 the firm specialised in selling cloth wholesale. And from those very earliest days the brothers were exporting Huddersfield made cloth all over the British Empire from their office and warehouse in Station Street.

Even at the beginning all kinds of cloth was marketed, all of it made in Huddersfield. A speciality however, was barathea cloth used in military uniforms by both British and French armed forces. For the uninitiated 'barathea' generally uses a worsted 'yarn' woven with a twill hopsack or broken rib weave. The resulting cloth has a fine texture with a slightly pebbled effect and faint regular twill lines running in opposite directions.

The firm moved to its present premises in Northumberland Street, in 1906, occupying a building which until then had been Huddersfield's main Post Office.

Two generations of the Dugdale family would follow the founding brothers in the business through good times and bad. Ironically for a company that specialised in material for military uniforms the war years of 1914-18 and 1939-1945 would prove particularly difficult, with Government restrictions on the sale of wool in the first world war, and clothes rationing in the second.

Top: *Dugdale archive:* ***Left:*** *Early advertising.* ***Below:*** *A Dugdale business card from 1937.*

December 24, 1937 1661 THE TAILOR AND CUTTER

ENGLAND'S CHOICEST SERGES

Pure Wool of Superior Quality.
Guaranteed Colours.
Durable and Delightful Wear.

Try the "UNIVERSITY" Serge. As a really reliable weighty cloth for "all the year round wear" it is unequalled.

DUGDALE BROS & CO LTD.
HUDDERSFIELD

Telephone: 1772 and 1773.
Telegrams: "Value, Huddersfield"

In the 1960s Keith Charnock joined the firm. He had begun his professional life as an apprentice at John Foster's in Queensbury. After National Service and a spell with his father at Kaye & Stewart, in Huddersfield, he switched to merchanting, joining the iconic firm J G Hardy.

Eighteen years after he joined the firm Keith Charnock bought Dugdales from Betty Dugdale the last of the Dugdale family in the business.

Keith's son, Rob Charnock, joined the company in 1990, and went on to acquire the firm from his father in 2000.

Today a wide range of different fabrics are sold throughout the world, though the firm still specialises in barathea cloth. Carefully selected yarns are bought in then sent out to selected weavers by the firm.

Customers are to be found in markets across the globe, not just in the former British Empire and in the Commonwealth, but in the USA, Europe, Brazil, Korea, Japan, the Far East and in the former Soviet Union countries. The highest quality worsted cloth combined with the firm's famed integrity, experience and skill are a winning formula. As a result Huddersfield cloth is much in demand, and appears in the very best of circles.

In 2011 rugby player Mike Tindall kicked off married life with Zara Phillips wearing a suit made from Huddersfield cloth supplied by Dugdales.

Dugdale Brothers supplied a classic black barathea for the morning suit which the England rugby star wore when he wed the Queen's grand-daughter and 12th in line to the throne on 30 July, 2011, in Edinburgh.

London bespoke tailors Cad & the Dandy were asked to kit out Mike and his male attendants for the big day – and immediately turned to their long-standing Huddersfield supplier.

The fathers of both the bride and the groom, as well as the ushers, were also kitted out by Cad & Dandy in the Huddersfield cloth supplied by Dugdales.

Even Hollywood it seems has now heard of Dugdales, with fabrics from the Huddersfield firm featuring in the 2011 Jim Carrey film, Mr Popper's Penguins.

Happily Dugdale Brothers has preserved its fabric archive created over several generations. It realises that bespoke tailors and designers worldwide share its vision that a past as rich in styles as it is in heritage is an invaluable inspiration for the future.

For that future the firm is developing an 'on-line' presence, enabling tailors in even the least likely parts of the world to order sample swatches of materials and access Dugdales famous fabrics for their own clients.

Top left, top right and above: *Then and now views of 5 Northumberland Street, home to the firm since 1906.* ***Left:*** *Rob Charnock pictured holding the finest Huddersfield cloth used to make Mike Tindall's suit for his marriage to Zara Phillips in 2011.*

Wood Auto Supplies - the Parts that Matter

Wood Auto Supplies Ltd, today based in Colne Road, was founded by Reginald Wood, originally trading as 'Wood the Battery Man'. The first Certificate of Incorporation is dated 1929, at the very start of the Great Depression.

Happily, one area of business which was less affected than most by the economic slump was the automotive industry. Reginald Wood had made a good choice when starting his own firm.

Reginald Wood would eventually become an influential force in the town and became Mayor of Huddersfield in the 1950s.

Reginald's home town was Huntingdon. Oliver Cromwell, too, hailed from Huntingdon, and, although the company moved its premises over the years they have all been named the 'Cromwell Works'.

After the war Reginald's two sons, John and Walter, began developing the merchandising side of the business. The firm moved to Portland Street, opposite the old Royal Infirmary. By now trading as Wood Auto Supplies Ltd, it concentrated on the manufacture of armatures, field coils, dynamos and starter motors.

The company expanded under John Wood and Douglas Heywood, who had been one of Reginald's first apprentices in 1930. In the meantime, Walter Wood developed the Factoring Division supplying local garages and fleet users with spare parts, accessories, paints and test equipment.

In 1952 the company took a stand at the Motor Show. Export opportunities followed, the first orders coming from Australia and Turkey.

The factory moved to Fitzwilliam Street in 1960 and finally to Colne Road in 1980 opposite sister company Wood Auto Factors Ltd, which supplies the local garage trade.

Last year Wood Auto exported to 85 countries and in recent years has formed alliances with overseas manufacturers to supplement the traditional homemade range to fit passenger cars, commercial and agricultural vehicles, marine and off-road applications of almost every make and model.

In 2007 Wood Auto acquired diesel injection specialist Leyland Auto Ltd so that today's group has over 120 employees and 100,000 sq ft of operations covering auto-electrical, diesel and also now vehicle air-conditioning products and processes.

Still a private independent company, Wood Auto has a long and proud history and has adapted confidently to modern demands in the ever more complex world of auto-electrical and diesel systems.

Top left: *Reginald Wood.* ***Left:*** *A Wood's display stand at the 1952 Earl's Court Motor Show.* ***Above:*** *An early view of the factory showing the efficiency and skill of the workers, an important factor in the continuing success of the company.* ***Below:*** *Wood's Cromwell Works.*

Phoenox Textiles - A Company On The Rise

Established in 1954, Phoenox Textiles Ltd, Spring Grove Mills, Clayton West, is a privately-owned family business. Today it is one of the UK's leading manufacturers/importers in the home textile industry. The company prides itself on offering quality products and services to major retailers across the world, backed by a highly talented team of dedicated professionals spread over manufacturing plants in the UK and India.

Phoenox are a relatively small company in a small community which makes them large employers. They have employed many second and even third generation families along the way. Their ethos is to employ from the local area where practical.

The company is home of the award winning brand 'Hug Rug' the world's most environmentally friendly barrier mat, manufactured entirely from recycled materials and exclusively made in Clayton West.

IMPROVED FOR 2010 –
New Colours & more Microfibre for even better dirt trapping ability...

The firm was founded by Jack Mosley, who worked as a weaver at Shelley Textiles before setting up Phoenox Textiles. Originally the firm made woven cloth for bus seating and traditional hearth rugs at Wood Street Mills. All materials were obtained locally, wool and acrylic from Yorkshire and cottons from Lancashire. Traditional machinery was used.

Today, by contrast, the firm uses modern Jet printing machines, automated tufting machines and even has its own backing plant in house. Yarn and materials are now sourced from all over the world.

Starting out with just ten staff, today the firm has some fifty employees at its 122,000 sq ft Spring Grove Mills where the company moved to in the late 1970s.

Jack Mosley's son David became very involved in the company along with cousins Melvyn and Michael Mosley.

David focused on production, creating new products, and getting major new contacts with mail order firms. He worked closely with Colin Hudson who concentrated on sales and marketing.

Jack Mosley died in 1975. He had been a traditional weaver who brought his hard earned expertise to the rug industry. He was involved in every aspect of the business. David followed in his father's footsteps on taking over management of the company.

David Mosley, well remembered for his renditions of 'Oh Danny Boy', was the main driving force behind the success of the business. Sadly, he passed way in 2007.

Phoenox is now run by the third generation of the family: Adrian Mosley, Charles Mosley and Steven Hirst, who now plan to expand the business through innovative product and design.

Top left: *Founder, Jack Mosley.* ***Left:*** *An early company vehicle from the 1950s.* ***Top right:*** *David Mosley.* ***Centre:*** *Phoenox's award winning 'Hug Rug' range.* ***Above:*** *Spring Grove Mills.*

Nelson Roller & Rubber Company - A Century of Progress

Vulcanisation, the treatment of rubber to give it qualities like strength, elasticity, and resistance to solvents was invented by American Charles Goodyear in 1839. Since then rubber has found thousands of applications, not least in Manchester Road, Linthwaite, where today the Nelson Roller & Rubber Company Ltd is based.

The business, originally located in Alfred Street, was founded by Robert Nelson in 1902. At his premises Robert and his staff covered spinning rollers in leather, and later cork, strips. Leather was softened with soap and ammonia. The strips were then stitched on to the rollers in what was in effect a cobbling operation. Leather eventually gave way to cork, which was glued on to the rollers.

Alfred Street remained the firm's home until the mid-1950s.

During the 1950s synthetic rubber and cork covering from the Armstrong Cork Company in the USA was introduced.

Company founder Robert Nelson was followed by his son George Stanley Nelson. But in 1965 Edwin Cusworth bought the business; he would in turn be followed by his son Martyn, and later his grandson, Julian Cusworth the present MD.

Today high speed rollers demand modern hi-tech materials to meet the needs of 21st century industry. With backing from its Colne Valley Polymers Division, Nelson Roller & Rubber is able to offer a broad range of roller coverings in different polymers and hardnesses.

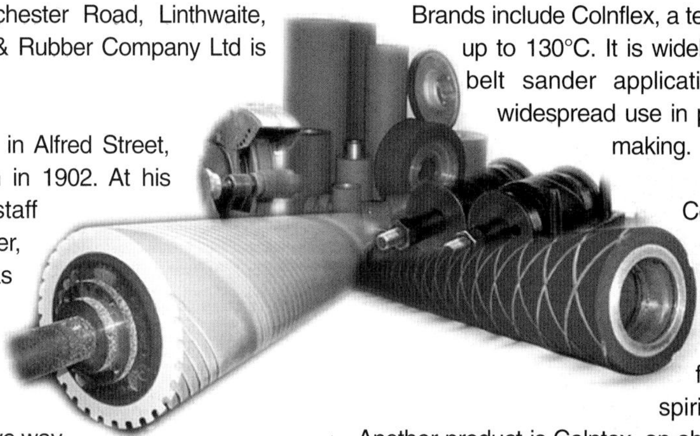

Brands include Colnflex, a terpolymer blend heat resistant up to 130°C. It is widely used in glue spreader and belt sander applications in woodworking, plus widespread use in polythene extrusion and bag-making.

Colnite is a highly sophisticated oil resistant rubber with high abrasion-resistance and heat resistance up to 170°C. Applications include friction feed wheels and hot white spirit and wax applications. Another product is Colntex, an abrasion and oil resistant textile roller covering designed to give good compression set and nip properties, but avoids swelling, sweating and deformation.

With over 100 years association with the textile trade during which time a vast range of compounds have been developed for combing, spinning and heat setting, every week thousands of kilos of yarn and top are being produced from rollers covered from Nelson's workshop. With this expertise and experience the future looks bright for Nelson Roller & Rubber Company.

Top: *Where it all began, Albert Sreet, pictured in the 1950s.*
Above: *A selection of rollers manufactured by the company.*

Above: Its seems hardly imaginable but the residents of Huddersfield were only able to access television from October 1951 when Holme Moss Transmitting Station began its service to an area covering 11 million people at the time. The base of the station is 1719 ft (524 m) above sea level and the mast another 750 ft (228 m) on top of that. This gives a maximum aerial height of 2467 ft (752 m) which is one of the highest in the UK. Television signals from Holme Moss travelled much further than their intended service area. The Isle of Man and parts of the Irish Republic, mainly Dublin and Wicklow, could receive a signal from Holme Moss for some years. Mr. P S Pearson, one of the broadcast engineers can be seen here checking the 'apology caption' which was used when there were transmission problems at the station and informed viewers that ' Normal Service would be resumed as soon as possible'.

Did you know?

Last of the Summer Wine, filmed in Holmfirth, was the longest-running comedy programme in Britain, and the longest running situation comedy in the world.

ACKNOWLEDGMENTS

The publishers would like to sincerely thank a number of individuals and organisations for their help and contribution to this publication.

Amanda Booth
Kirklees Image Archive, Tolson Museum Huddersfield
www.kirkleesimages.org.uk

Huddersfield Examiner

Morris Bray